Options Trading For Beginners:

Crash Day Course to Become a Profitable Investor in Your Spare Time for a Living with Strategies to Trade Penny Stocks, Bond, EFT, Futures & Forex Markets in 7 Days

ROBERT ZONE

Table of Contents

Introduction

Chapter 1. Understanding Option Trading

Chapter 2 How to Start Options Trading

Chapter 3 Brokers

Chapter 4 Platforms and Tools for Options Trading

Chapter 5 Basic Investment Strategies

Chapter 6 How Options Are Priced

Chapter 7 Risk Management

Chapter 8 The Basics Of Technical Analysis

Chapter 9 Trading psychology

Chapter 10 The Best Strategies to Make Money

Chapter 11 Tips for Success

Conclusion

© **Copyright 2019 - All rights reserved.**

The content contained within this book may not be reproduced, duplicated or transmitted without direct written permission from the author or the publisher.

Under no circumstances will any blame or legal responsibility be held against the publisher, or author, for any damages, reparation, or monetary loss due to the information contained within this book. Either directly or indirectly.

Legal Notice:

This book is copyright protected. This book is only for personal use. You cannot amend, distribute, sell, use, quote or paraphrase any part, or the content within this book, without the consent of the author or publisher.

Disclaimer Notice:

Please note the information contained within this document is for educational and entertainment purposes only. All effort has been executed to present accurate, up to date, and reliable, complete information. No warranties of any kind are declared or implied. Readers acknowledge that the author is not engaging in the rendering of legal, financial, medical or professional advice. The content within this book has been derived from various sources. Please consult a licensed professional before attempting any techniques outlined in this book.

By reading this document, the reader agrees that under no circumstances is the author responsible for any losses, direct or indirect, which are incurred as a result of the use of information contained within this document, including, but not limited to, — errors, omissions, or inaccuracies.

Introduction

If you were to find an investor and ask to look at their portfolio, you will be able to see that they have a large variety of investments that they are working on. They don't just put all their money on one company all the time. Instead they have many different types of investments they can work with such as bonds, stocks, mutual funds, and more. In addition, there are times when a portfolio will include options, but it is not as likely to be there as some of the others.

This is like getting a key where once you use that key to open the front door of a house, then it belongs to you. You may not technically own the house because you have the key, but you can use that key whenever you would like and if you choose, you could purchase the house later on.

Options are set up so that they cost you a certain fixed price for so much time. This length will change based on the option that you are working with. Sometimes you will have an option that only lasts for a day and then there are some that you may hold onto for a few years. You will know how long the option is going to last before you make the purchase.

Options are nothing new. It's a well-known term in trading, and even though it might be overwhelming for some people to think about, options are not really hard to understand. The portfolios of investors are generally composed of different classes of assets, which can be bonds, mutual funds, stocks or even ETFs. One such asset class are options, and certain advantages are offered by them when used accurately, which other trading stocks and ETFs cannot offer. Like many other asset classes, options too can be purchased with brokerage investment accounts.

Options can be considered as an investment that gives you more "options."

But that does not mean that there are no risks involved. Almost every investment entails a multitude of risks. The same goes for options. An investor ought to know of these risks before proceeding with trade.

Options are a part of the group of securities called derivatives. The term derivative is many a time associated with huge risks and volatile performance. Warren Buffett once called derivatives "weapons of mass destruction," which is a little too much.

Options are a kind of derivative. Investors are often talking about different derivatives. Options derive their value from an underlying stock or security. In fact, options belong to the class of securities known as derivatives. For a long time, people associated derivatives with high-risk investments. This notion is not really true.

Derivatives obtain their value from an underlying security. Think about wine, for instance. Wine is produced from grapes. We also have ketchup which is derived from tomatoes. This is basically how derivatives function.

One can gain a real advantage in the market if they know how options work and can use them properly since you can put the cards in your favor if you can use options correctly. The great thing about options is that you can use them according to your style. If you're a speculative person, earn through speculation. If not, earn without speculating. You should know how options work even if you decide never to use them because other companies you invest in might use options.

Options are an attractive investment tool. They have a risk/reward framework, which is unlike any other. They can be used in a multitude of combinations that make them very versatile. The risk factor involved can be diluted by using these options with other financial instruments or other option contracts, and at the same time opening more avenues for profits. While many investments have an unbound quantum of risk attached, options' trading, on the other hand, has defined risks, which the buyers know about.

Chapter 1

Understanding Option Trading

Now, there are several options that will work when you are dealing with options. Some of the ones that you will come across on a regular basis include:

- Bonds: A bond is going to be a debt investment where the investor is able to loan out their money to the government or company. Then this money will be used for a variety of projects by the second party. But at some time, usually determined when the money is given over, the money will be paid back along with some interest. Most of the time you will work with a government bond and these bonds are even found on the public exchange.
- Commodity: Commodities are another choice that you can make when you are working with options. These will be any basic goods that will be used in commerce and can include some choices like beef, oil, and grain. When you trade these, there will be a minimum of quality that they must meet.

These are popular because commodities are considered tangible, which means that they represent something that is real.

- Currency: Currency is going to talk about any type of money that is accepted by the government and can include coins and paper money. Of course, cryptocurrency and Bitcoin are starting to join the market as well. The exchange rate of these currencies, especially when it comes to the digital currencies, will change quite a bit in very little time so it is important to be careful with these.
- Futures: These are going to be similar to what you found with commodities, but they have some different guidelines on how they can be delivered, the quantity and quality, and more.
- Index: An index is going to be a group of securities that are imaginary and will symbolize the statistical measurement of how those will do in the market.
- Stock: You can own a certain percentage of the share, but instead of running that company, you will let other management do

that while you make some profits each quarter when the company does well.

Options may sound complex but are pretty easy to understand if you pay keen attention. You will come across numerous traders' profiles with different security types including bonds, stocks, mutual funds, ETFs, and even options.

Options are another asset class. If applied correctly, they will offer numerous benefits that all other assets on their own cannot. For instance, you can use options to hedge against negative outcomes like a declining stock market or falling oil prices. You can use options to generate recurrent income and for speculative purposes like wagering on the movement of a stock.

When Should You Use Options?

As an investor, you will have a number of opportunities to use options. However, there is a number that is truly beneficial. Here is a brief look at them.

- Options buy you time if you need to sit back and watch things develop.

- You require very little funds to invest in options compared to buying shares.

- Options will offer you protection from losses because they lock in price but without the obligation to buy.

Always keep in mind that options offer no free ride or a free lunch. Trading in options carries some risks due to their predictive nature. Any prediction will turn out one way or another. The good news here is that any losses that you incur will only be equivalent to the cost of setting up the option. This cost is significantly lower than buying the underlying security.

Differentiating Options from Stocks

While there is no expiration date in stocks, Options contract has one. This expiration period can be as long as a week or months or even years, and it is determined by the kind of options you are practicing and other related regulations.

Stocks are not a part of derivatives, while options are which means their value is derived from something else.

While stocks are a well-defined numerical quantity, options are not.

One can even profit with a drop in prices of the underlying stock, which is dependent on the type of strategy they are following.

Stock owners have a right in the company either for dividend or voting or both. Options owners have no such rights.

Types of Options

There are various types of options from which a trader can take advantage that will then allow him or her to sell or buy options. In addition to this, there are subcategories of options with different stipulations and advantages. It is important to review and be familiar with these in order to use options for maximum profit. Traders would do well to remember that options trading does take a lot of practice and only those who are well versed in options trading and aware of the movement and trends of companies and financial institutions do well in this particular sect of trading. That being said, here are the various categories of options trading.

Calls

Calls are used by buyers, meaning that if a trader has a call option, they have the right, but are not obligated, to buy an underlying asset at the strike price before a previously agreed upon expiration date. A call option is a contract or agreement that gives the investor/holder the right – but not obligation – to Purchase an asset at a specified price within a specified time. The main difference is that the call option gives you the right to buy or call in asset. When the price of the asset increases, you can gain a profit from a call.

The writer of the call option, also referred to as the seller, has an obligation to sell the security/asset if the investor exercises the option. The seller receives a premium for taking on the risk associated with the obligation.

Puts

The catch for the seller is that the price will need to drop before the expiration date. If this occurs, then the buyer will likely have paid the seller the full strike price, which will be more than the value of the asset. If the price plummets after the expiration date however, the seller will only gain the initial options premium used to secure the contract. Unfortunately, this also means the seller is probably losing money on the underlying asset, which they still own. However, if the seller writes a put as part of a strategy, they will need to keep in mind that the put can always be assigned and the investor will be forced to sell. In regards to the –in, -at, and –out-of-the-money terms, the exact opposite of calls is true of puts.

Before moving on to the other types of options, here is a quick note concerning some brief clarification regarding those who participate in options trading. There are four positions that can be held that fall into two categories. The first category is made up the "holders," and includes those who buy calls and puts.

This option gives a buyer the right to SELL an asset/security at a given strike price before the date of expiry. The writer/seller of the option has an obligation to purchase the security/asset if the strike price is exercised.

How option trading works

There are several parties involved in a trade. It isn't possible to trade directly with everyone, and it isn't even practical. This is why, for the sake of convenience, stock exchanges were formed. This is a channel where all the stocks are being traded.

You cannot work directly with the stock exchange as this would create great confusion. It would mean too many people making deals at the same time. This is where brokers come into play.

Brokers work as the mediators, as the channel of communication between you and the exchange. They charge a commission for their service. In the stock exchange industry's early stages, most of the transactions were carried out by the brokers on behalf of their clients. Brokers nowadays still carry out transactions on behalf of their clients, but the clients now have the option to manage their accounts easily. You will have to open a trading account with a broker, and the broker will give you access to that trading account.

Currently, a number of software programs have been successfully developed where you can directly trade on stock exchanges. The program recommendation, as well as the access credentials, will be provided by the brokerage firm you'll choose.

Like a bond or stock, an option is a tradable security. You can purchase or sell options to a foreign broker or trade them on an exchange within the United States. An option may give you the opportunity to leverage your cash, though it may be high risk because it eventually expires *(expiration date)*. For stock options, each option contract represents 100 shares.

An instance of an option is if you want to buy a car/house, but for whatever reason, do not have immediate cash for it but will get the cash next month. You can now buy the asset at the agreed price and sell it for a profit. The value of the asset may also depreciate perhaps when the house develops plumbing problems or other problems or in the case of a vehicle, gets into an accident. If you decide not to buy the asset and let your purchase option expire, you lose your initial investment, the $2,500 you placed for the option.

This is the general concept of how option trading happens; however, in reality, option trading is a lot more complex and involves more risks.

What kind of investor are you?

Trading has its strategies, its techniques and its secrets. Different things apply to different people. What works for someone else may not work for you. Why? Because you are two different kinds of investors. Aggressive personalities invest in a completely different manner than conservative personalities. People who are not afraid to take risks are completely different investors than those who are methodical and play it safe. There is no better or worse here. It is just the style of doing business.

There are two major categories of investors:

- **The active investor** Those are also called traders. They do not hold on to options for a long time and their interest lies in making profit from the volatility of the prices. The trade a lot and as often as possible.

- **The passive investor** These are also called the buy-and-hold investors. They are the exact opposites. They are interested in making the maximum gain from each option and they do not trade often. And when they do they will trade once or twice.

Most people could find themselves at any point between those two categories. Some tend to be more aggressive, others tend to be slightly more conservative. One would think that being in the middle would offer you the best of both. But this is not always the case.

Aggressive personalities are actually impatient personalities. For them patience is not a virtue. So if you force them to trade conservatively in most cases they do not even know how. And they do not care to learn. The same holds true for the conservative people. Forcing them to trade more options than one or two, creates a chaos in their mindset.

Each one balances to whichever side they feel more comfortable. The side that will allow him or her to think straight and make the proper decisions. That would be the perfect world, but unfortunately there are always strings attached.

Even the most conservative investor may have to act fast and trade all his options should an emergency arise. An aggressive person should learn that there are cases where trading may be forbidden, or banned, or halted for some reason and they will have to hold on to their options.

The deeper you get into options trading the wiser you become. No matter what kind of investor you may be, the market itself will teach you, sometimes the hard way (i.e. it will cost you a lot of money) when it is time to hold on to an option and when it is time to trade it.

Top Reasons to Trade in Options

Limit Your Risk

A good reason to go with buying options is that you will be able to limit your risk down to just the amount of money that you pay for the premium. With other investment options, you could end up losing a lot of money, even money that you did not invest to begin with, but this does not happen when you are working with options.

Higher Percentage of Returns

As mentioned, an options trader is only going to pay a fraction of the value of the asset just to have some control over that asset. This will allow the trader to earn more money than what they would be able to earn when they purchase the asset upfront and then try to sell it.

Helps to Hedge Intraday or Futures Trades

It is common for traders to purchase or short-sell Futures contracts because they expect them to move in one direction or another. You may not be complaining when this goes the right way and you earn unlimited profits, but if you go with one of these trades and you don't hedge your position, you are going to complain when you start losing a lot of money. If you have an understanding on how trading options works, you could buy call or put options to help insure that you are not going to end up with an unlimited loss. The right options choice is going to help control your loss the moment that the intraday or futures positions starts going against what you wanted.

Options are flexible

When you are working with options, you will find that you get a ton of flexibility. You can choose to buy or sell, you can go with different expiration dates, you can pick from a variety of strategies and assets, and you can even have control over your strike price. There are even ways that you will be able to profit if the market goes down. Sometimes all this flexibility is going to make working in options more complicated, but if you know what you are doing, this type of flexibility will help you to profit, regardless of how the market is doing.

Gain leverage

Another benefit you will be able to get when you decide to work with the options market is the idea of leverage. To keep things simple, leverage is a big advantage to the trader. When you gain leverage, you are giving yourself more options because you are able to put more money into the market without needing to have more startup capital to help you out. This can be dangerous because it causes you to lose more money than you have in the beginning, but if you are careful and read the market right, it will make you earn a ton more money even with lower startup costs.

Low-risk

You will find that working with options can be relatively low risk. First, these options are more affordable than what you are able to get with some other types of investing, so you are limiting the risks that you are taking, as long as you use the right strategies as you do it. You are even able to look at some of the trades and pick the ones that have less risk so that you will lose less, even if the trade doesn't go the way that you want.

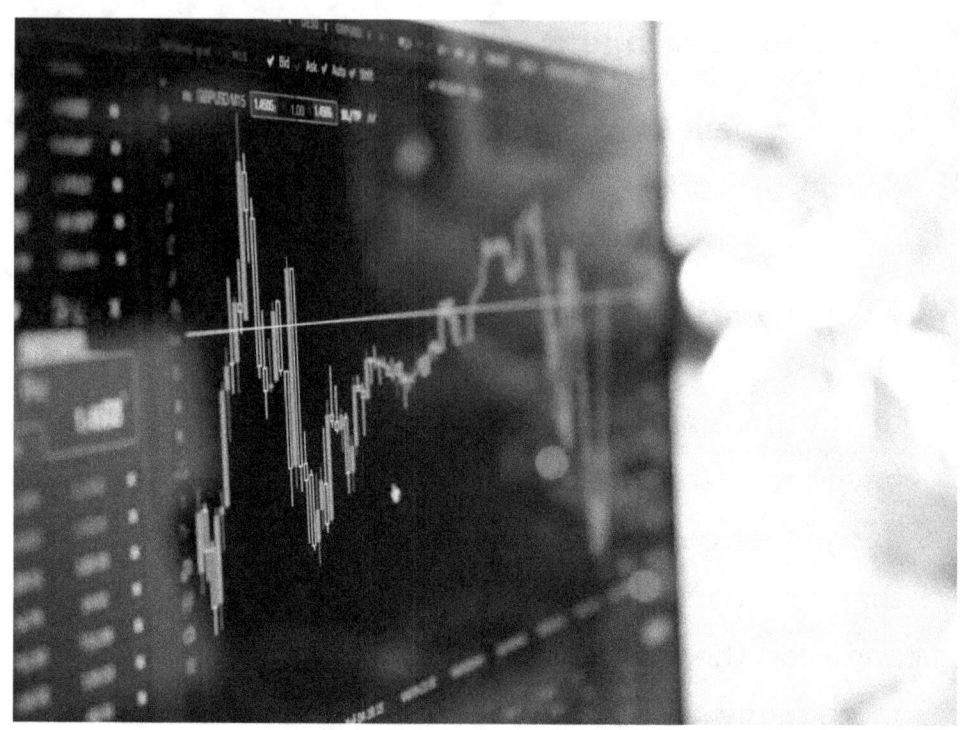

Chapter 2
How to Start Options Trading

There is always a beginning of everything we do in life. In this chapter, I will take you through on some of the ways on how to start options trading, some of the strategies needed for newbies of options trading, and also, the capital needed to start on this type of trading.

How Much Capital Is Needed?

After knowing how options trading works, do not rush to waste on your cash. There are too many risks in this type of trading. Capital is a basic requirement to start any business. Does options trading require too much capital? No. When starting on options trading, it is better to start with small capital to avoid massive trading risks.

Many are the individuals who utilize much of their cash for trading during their first days, which is so dangerous. Such individuals end up having too many risks to handle, and finally, they make up their minds to close their businesses. I do not want you to fall into such a mess. Do your thing with the right speed.

Start options trading with a reasonable small amount. Do not brag off that you got everything under control. You will lose even the only cash you had. Starting with less money has a high likelihood of fewer risks in trading. I bet you can now handle a few risks and be able to continue with your trading.

Strategies Used by Beginners for Options Trading

Options trading has a wide variety of strategies. There are simple to complex strategies that you can implement in options trading. Beginners find it tough to know the best simple strategies to utilize in their trading. You do not need to worry anymore. I have provided a detailed list below of the different simple options trading strategies you can use:

Buying calls. Buying calls is the simplest options trading strategy for beginners, investors, and even professionals. Investors prefer calls so much because this strategy provides them with the honor to purchase stock at a certain agreed price with a minimum amount of capital within an agreed time before its expiry.

Most of the bullish traders use this options strategy. When there is a rise in the price of the stock, you earn good profits. This strategy is right for any beginner who wants to generate better income, earn huge profits, and even save on the trading capital.

Its great potential to massive profits, however, makes it have a bigger exposure to the trading risks. You, as a buyer, can know the risks involved in your trading. Also, buying a call strategy has a better and secure feature, which can handle many risks.

The major drawback of purchasing calls is associated with the time of expiry and the loss of value. They always have a time of expiry, so you need to check on the timing. Call options lose their value when their time of expiry reaches. You do not earn any dividends when your options are past the date of expiry.

Buying put. Buying put is another simple strategy, which is just the vice versa of buying calls. Most investors use this expecting the stock's price will fall within that time before expiry. Investors always gain good enough profits when their prediction becomes right.

The things to put into consideration when buying put options include the time you are planning to be on trade and the amount of money you can afford to buy options. Purchase put options with at least one month remaining for them to expire. Do not purchase an option with a long duration before it expires. It will lose its time premium. You do not need to buy options with a duration like one year remaining for them to expire, because you will not wait to trade an option for a whole year. So, be wise when buying options.

The other consideration is all about buying options that you can afford. Do not torture yourself by buying expensive put options. You will get hurt at the end. Weigh the different prices of the put options available and select the one you can afford according to the risks involved and the size of your account.

In case their prediction fails, the loss associated with this strategy is so limited. Unfortunately, you become exposed to so many risks.

Short put. Short put options strategy is all about buying a stock at a lower price than its current cost in the market. You gain profits in situations where the stock's price remains above an agreed price within that time of expiry. Otherwise, you incur many losses.

Conversely, in situations where the stock's price falls below the price agreed before the time of expiration, another party on trade sells you the stock at the agreed price, and you have to buy it no matter the cost.

Selling a short put option is quite simple, look for a margin account and a stock that will not drop its value any time soon. Select a date of expiration that is not that far and agree on the right price to generate more income when selling. By the time of expiry comes, you will earn good profits as long as the price does not fall.

You should be extra cautious when implementing this strategy, or else, you may lose value in your trading when things turn out unexpectedly.

Covered call. A covered call is one of the preferred options strategies for beginners. It is mostly suitable for traders who have expectations of small changes in the price of the stock or no changes at all within the expected time of expiry. A trader using this strategy normally purchases around 100 shares (unit of capital) of the stock and sells a call option against the unit of capital.

After selling the option, you acquire option premiums and decrease the cost of the share. If the price of the asset behaves unexpectedly in the market, meaning that it becomes greater than an agreed price, there should be the sale of the asset by the owner using the agreed price.

Married put. A married put is an options trading strategy quite similar to the insurance policies we normally have at our homes. The strategy enables an investor who owns a stock, to purchase a put option on the stock to protect it against loss in value in the price of the stock.

You should buy the stock and put options on the same day. Also, you need to inform the options broker that the delivery of the stock you purchased will happen after the exercise of the put option. Marriage put strategy is normally used by bullish traders when buying their market trades who want to shield themselves from unlimited losses.

The drawback of this strategy is that it is costly to implement it on your trading portfolio.

Cash-secured put. On this strategy, traders write put options, and at the same time, put aside a sufficient amount of cash for buying stock. The benefits of this strategy are that you can decide on the price you want when you implement this strategy. Also, you receive payment of the options premiums when you sell cash-secured put options. In situations where the stock's price falls below an agreed price, the trader incurs too many losses.

Protective put. A protective put is an options trading strategy that many bullish traders implement to shield against loss of an asset, which is mostly caused by the drop in the price of an asset. A trader holds on to the long position of a stock and then buys a put option at an agreed price closer or equal to the price of the stock.

if it declines, the put options normally protect the agreed price (strike price) within that duration until the time of expiry. Remember, options have a date of expiration.

In scenarios where the price of the stock rises, the trader involved gains good enough profits. However, the profits reduce in cases of the options cost and also commissions. Another drawback of buying puts is that the total cost of the put normally surges due to the cost of the options.

You are supposed to offer the put options for sale in scenarios where the agreed price becomes greater than the stock's price after the time of expiry. However, this leaves the asset unprotected. Alternatively, a trader can also offer the put options for sale and purchase other options.

Collar strategy. Moderate bullish traders who formulate this strategy hold shares of an asset while at the same time, purchase put options and offer call options for sale. Both the put options and call options in collar strategy have a similar time of expiry.

It is also applicable to traders who are just writing covered calls to earn premiums and also want to protect themselves from the unexpected decline in the price of a stock.

A collar strategy normally limits losses in trading but also, unfortunately, limits the gaining of huge profits. You can make more profits without this strategy in cases where the price of the stock rises.

Now, with the idea of the simple options trading strategies that exist, you should sit down, think, and select the best strategy to use as a beginner. Weigh the risks and rewards of the strategy you will choose for excellent performance in options trading.

How to Start Options Trading

Now with the basic knowledge on options trading, I will provide you with a few details on how to start options trading journey.

1. You should look for an options trading broker. The key to successful options trading is your broker. There exist legit and non-legit brokers in options trading. Some of the tips for selecting a good broker include the following:
   - Do some research on the broker first. You need to be keen and alert before opening a brokerage options trading platform. Different brokers will approach you with different platforms. Do not rush or assume everything

is good; do some research on the best brokers. Make sure you spend your cash well by paying for a good options trading platform. It will help you a lot because your trading performance depends on your platform. Choose a broker with good ratings.

- Charges lower commissions. Some brokers tend to exploit traders by charging high commissions to beginners. You should weigh different commission offers of different brokers before settling on one. Some even charge no commission to traders. You should prefer brokers with fewer commissions. Payment of high commissions periodically can mess you up with losses, and you may find it even hard to secure your trading capital. Do not accept to pay high commissions. You also need to do some savings other than wasting money while paying commissions.

- A simple user interface platform. There is a wide variety of software with different functionalities and features. Some software has a simple user interface, while others are too complex for you to use. You should choose a platform with a simple and clear user interface that enables you to do your trades with less struggle. Some platforms can waste your precious time when you struggle too much searching on the Internet on how you operate them. Make your work easier by handling software that is according to your level.

- Trading tools for research. You should also consider factors like tools that are present on the platform. Do not purchase a platform with no tools. It will be hard for you. Platform tools ease your trading and make your performance excellent. The tools here may include charting tools, research tools, and even tools that alert you on any market changes that may arise.
- Do some testing on the brokerage platform. Do not be that kind of a careless trader who does things for the sake of doing with no precautions. You need to be cautious enough since this is an income-generating activity. You should test on a brokerage

software before making up your mind of purchasing it. Check on the reliability and stability of the software and be 100% sure that this is the platform you will use for your trading. Ensure the software is not that type of platform that crashes down unexpectedly. You might miss crucial trade while fixing your software.

2. Be approved to trade options. You need to be approved by the broker in charge before purchasing and offering options for sale. They normally have their ways of approving you, like checking your experience and the money that you have. It aids in avoiding risks for the customers. You cannot escape this step.

3. Get a clear understanding of the technical analysis. Options trading is a technical field. You need to have the technical analysis techniques of trading options. The technical aspects include reading charts, know about the volume of stock, and also moving averages. Trading charts mostly analyze price behavior in the market. You will handle the aspects many times while trading.

Perfect your technical knowledge and be cautious with them.

4. Take advantage of mock trading accounts. Using real accounts when starting options trading is a risky game. You can lose a lot of cash within a short time duration. Mock accounts exist for a reason. You should test your trading skills in the mock accounts, learn a few tricks, and perfect your skills. The advantage of using a mock account is that there is no loss of money since they mostly provide virtual money. It prepares you for real trading. You should take advantage of them and learn a lot. Utilize them for a while and do some evaluations on your returns. When everything works out well, face real trading and shine.

5. Utilize limit orders. It is risky to rely on market prices since price behavior change with time. You should utilize limit orders when trading. A limit order is a type of order that enables you to purchase market securities at an agreed price. Using this type of order shuns you from incurring losses in options trading.

6. Revise your strategies with time. After entering into the options trading, with time, you need to revise your strategies. Utilize the working strategies more often and get rid of unsuccessful trading strategies. You should not have many strategies that do not bring good performance. Few working strategies are better than having multiple ones that do not help you.
7. Register and join in options trading platforms. Joining forums comprised of other options traders is another way of how to get started in options trading. Forums are platforms of different people with different experiences and opinions. You can learn mistakes made by others in trading. It is part of growing in options trading. So why shouldn't you give it a try?
8. Study and learn about trading metrics. Having your returns maximized is also another way of getting started in options trading. Traders normally use different trading metrics such as delta, gamma, theta, and vega. You should learn and practice them for massive returns.

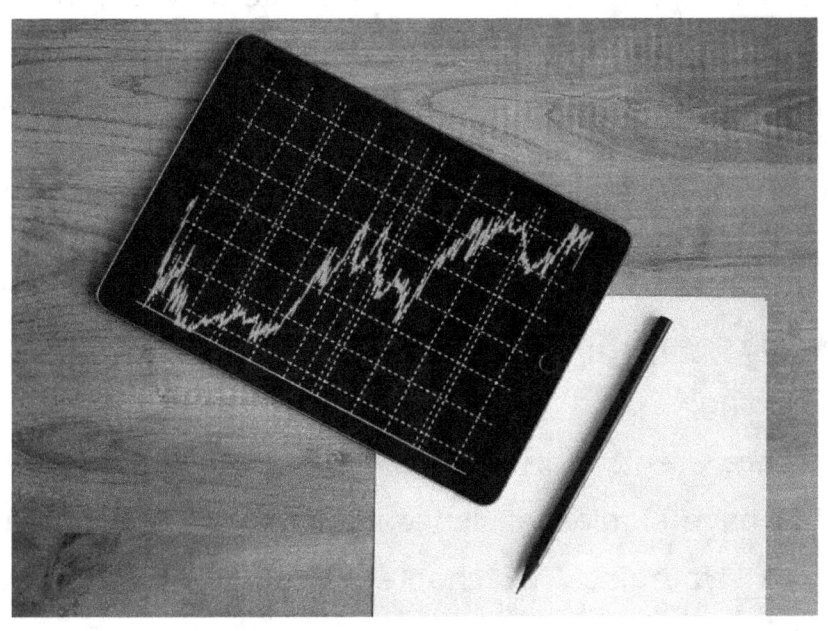

Chapter 3   Brokers

When it comes to selecting brokers, you have many options available. There are full service, discount, online, etc. Understanding the differences between them and selecting the ones best suited for your purposes is crucial if you wish to succeed. Another area that a lot of beginners ignore and then receive a rude lesson in is the regulations surrounding options trading.

There aren't too many rules to comply with, but they do have significant consequences for your capital and risk strategies. This chapter is going to fill you in on all the details.

Choosing a Broker

Generally speaking, there are two major varieties of brokers: Discount and full service. In fact, a lot of full-service brokers have discount arms these days so you will see some overlap. Full service refers to an organization where brokerage is just a part of a larger financial supermarket.

The broker might offer you other investment solutions, estate planning strategies, and so on. They'll also have an in house research wing which will send you reports to help you trade better. In addition to this, they'll also have phone support in case you have any questions or wish to place an order.

Once you develop a good relationship with them, a full-service broker will become a good organization to network. Every broker loves a profitable customer since it helps with marketing. A full-service broker will have good relationships in the industry and if you have specific needs, they can put you in touch with the right people.

The price of all this service is you paying higher commissions than average. It is up to you to see whether this is a good price for you to pay. As such, you don't need to signup with a full-service broker to trade successfully. Order matching is done electronically so it's not as if a person on the floor can get you a better price these days. Therefore, a full-service house is not going to give you better execution.

Discount brokers, on the other hand, are all about focus. They help you trade, and that is it. They will not provide advice, at least not intentionally from a business perspective, and phone ordering is nonexistent. That doesn't mean customer service is reduced. Far from it.

Commissions will be lower as well, far lower than what you can expect to pay at a full-service house. The downside of a discount brokerage is that you're not going to receive any special product recommendations or solutions outside of your speculative activities. A lot of people prefer to trade (using a separate account) with the broker they have their retirement accounts with so everything is kept in-house.

So which one should you choose? Well, if you aim to keep costs as low as possible, then select a discount broker. In fact, only in the case where you're keen on keeping things in one place should you choose a full-service broker. These days, there's no difference between the two options otherwise.

An exception here is if you have a large amount of capital, north of half a million dollars. In such cases, a full-service broker will be cheaper because of their volume-based commission offers. You'll pay the same rate or as close to what a discount broker would charge you, and you get all the additional services. Whatever additional amounts you need to invest can be handled by the firm through their wealth management line of business.

There are a few terms you must understand, no matter which broker you choose so let's look at these now.

Margin

Margin refers to the number of assets you currently hold in your account. Your assets are cash and positions. As the market value of your positions fluctuates, so does the amount of margin you have. Margin is an important concept to grasp since it is at the core of your risk management discipline.

When you open an account with your broker, you will have a choice to make. You can open either a cash or margin account. In order to trade options, you have to open a margin account. Briefly, a cash account does not include leverage within it, so all you can trade are stocks. There are no account minimums for a cash account, and even if they are, they're pretty minuscule.

A margin account, on the other hand, is subject to very different rules. First, the minimum balances for a margin account are higher. Most brokers will impose a $10,000 minimum, and some will even increase this amount based on your trading style. The account minimum doesn't achieve anything by itself, but it acts as a commitment of sorts for the broker.

The thinking is that with this much money on the line, the person trading is going to be a bit more serious about it and won't blow it away. If only it worked like that. Anyway, the minimum balance is a hard and fast rule. Another rule you should be aware of is the Pattern Day Trader (PDT) designation.

PDT is a rule that comes directly from the SEC. Anyone who executes four or more orders within five days is classified as a PDT ("Pattern Day Trader," 2019). One this tag is slapped onto you, your broker is going to ask you to post at least $25,000 in the margin as a minimum balance. Again, this minimum balance doesn't do anything but the SEC figures that if you do screw up, this gives you enough of a buffer.

Will the strategies in this book get you classified as a PDT? Well, this depends on you. Each strategy by itself plays out over a month or more so once you enter, all you need to do is monitor it and if you want, you can adjust it. However, if you're going to avoid the PDT, you're limited to entering just three positions per workweek.

My advice is to study the strategies and to start slowly. Trade just one instrument at first and see how it goes and then expand once you gain more confidence. At that point, you'll have enough experience to figure out how much capital you need. Remember that even exiting a position is considered a trade, so PDT doesn't refer just to trade entry.

Margin Call

One other aspect of margin you must understand is the margin call. This is a dreaded message for most traders, including institutional ones. The purpose of all risk management is to keep you as far away as possible from this ever happening to you. A margin call is issued when you have inadequate funds in your account to cover its requirements.

Remember that your margin is the combination of the cash you hold plus the value of your positions. If you have $1000 in cash, but your position is currently in a loss of -$900, you'll receive a margin call to post more cash to cover the potential loss you're headed for. In fact, you'll receive it well in advance. If you don't post more margin, your broker has the right to close out your positions and recover whatever cash they can to stop their risk limits from being triggered.

The threshold beyond which your broker will issue a margin call is called the maintenance margin. Usually, you need to maintain 25% of your initial position value (that is when you enter a position) as cash in your account. Most brokers have a handy indicator which tells you how close you are to the limit.

The leading cause of margin calls is leverage. With a margin account, you can borrow money from your broker and use that to boost your returns. Let's look at an example: if you trade with $10,000 of your own money and borrow $20,000 from your broker to enter a position, you control $30,000 worth of the position. Let's say this position makes a gain of $10,000 to bring its total value to $40,000.

You've just made a 100% return on this investment (since you invested just $10,000) despite the total return on the position is 33% (10,000/30,000). What happens if you lose $10,000 on the position though? Well, you just lost 100% despite the position losing only 33%. Leverage is a double-edged sword.

It is far too simplistic to call leverage bad or good. It is what it is. If you're a beginner, you should not be borrowing money to trade under any circumstances. When you're experienced, you can choose to do so as much as you want. Please note, I'm differentiating between the leverage where you borrow money, and the sort of leverage options provide.

With options, a single contract gives you control over a larger pie of stock, but the option premium still needs to be paid. It is, therefore, cheaper to trade options than the common stock. If you were to borrow money to pay for the option premium, then you're indulging in foolish behavior, and you need to step away.

There's a difference between leverage being inherent within the structure of the instrument and using leverage to increase the amount of something you can buy. The latter should be avoided when you're a beginner.

Execution

A favorite pastime of unsuccessful traders is to complain about execution. Their losses are always the broker's fault, and if it weren't for the greedy brokers, they'd be rolling in the dough, diving in and out of it like Scrooge McDuck. Complaining about your execution will get you nothing. A big reason for these complaints is that most beginner traders don't realize that the price they see on the screen is not the same as what is being traded on the exchange.

We live in an era of high-frequency trading, and the markets' smallest measurement of time has gone from seconds to microseconds. Trades are constantly pouring in, and the matching engine is always finding suitable sellers for buyers. Given the pace of the market, it is important to understand that it is humanly impossible to figure out the exact price of an instrument.

Therefore, within your risk management plan, you must make allowance for times of high volatility when the fluctuations will be bigger. For now, I want you to understand that just because the price you received was different from what was on screen doesn't mean the broker is incompetent.

How do you identify an incompetent broker? Customer service and the quality of the trading terminal they give you access to are the best indicators. Your broker is not in the game to trade against you or fleece you. Admittedly, this is not the case with FX, but we're not discussing FX in this book. So stop blaming your broker and look at your systems instead, assuming the broker passes basic due diligence.

When it comes to placing orders with your broker, you have many options. There are different order types you can place, and each order has a specific purpose. First off, we have the market order. This is the simplest order to understand. When you place a market order, you're telling your broker to fill your entire order at whatever price they can find on the market.

A market order usually results in fast fills, unless there's a volatility event of some sort going on. The next type of order you can place is the limit order. The limit prioritizes order price over quantity. For example, if you want to enter 100 units of an instrument at $10, your broker will buy as much as possible under or equal to $10. If they can get just 90 units under $10, then that's it.

A limit order works for a lot of traders looking to enter a position. Directional risk management depends a lot on the size of the position, so it is critical not to exceed the positions limit. For such traders, this is a beneficial order. The last type of order you will encounter is the stop order. The stop prioritizes quantity over price.

Stop orders have a trigger attached to them, and once market price hits the trigger, the entire quantity of the order is executed, irrespective of what the price is. Stop orders are very useful to get out of positions quickly. Indeed, the stop-loss order is a stop order with the 'loss' in the name simply referring to the minimization of losses in case the trade goes south.

Another order you should be aware of is the Good Till Cancelled or GTC. A cousin of the GTC is the Day order. These two do not order types as much as expiry conditions for the order. A GTC is valid until the trader explicitly cancels it while the day order cancels itself at the end of the market session.

All in all, there are over a hundred different types of order your average broker offers you. Do not get bogged down trying to figure them all out. Institutional traders use most of them for specific strategies. To trade well, you don't need to understand a single word of what those orders are about. Stick to the ones mentioned here, and you can trade successfully.

The question now is, how and where should you use these orders? Well since you're trading options, you're not going to be too concerned with stop losses and your exits are going to involve letting options expire. Thus, the biggest concern you should have is with regard to trade entry.

With options, you can choose either market or limit orders to enter. Personally, I favor market orders since it guarantees you an entry. Risk management here is a bit different than with directional trades so you can afford to enter at the market. The only exception is if there are extreme volatility conditions present.

Price Quotes

A lot of traders are stumped when they first look at their trading screens and see that there are two prices for everything. After all, every financial channel always displays one price for security but when trading, you'll be quoted two different prices within the price box. This is a small but crucial detail for you to understand.

The lower price you receive is called the bid, and this is the price you will pay if you sell the instrument. The higher price is the ask, and this is what you will pay to buy the instrument. The single price you see on your TV screen is the "Last Traded Price" or LTP. Do not make the mistake of thinking the LTP is the real price since the market moves constantly.

In fact, even the spread (the difference between the ask and the bid) doesn't accurately reflect the true state of things thanks to constant movement. There's no need to be alarmed though, as long as volatility is stable, the difference isn't much. Just remember to look at the spread to understand what you'll be paying. The spread increases and contracts constantly but if you see that it is getting too big, this is a sign that too much volatility exists and you're better off staying out.

This concludes our look at brokers and the ins and outs of it. As you can see, there isn't too much to be concerned about, but you need to be well aware since it impacts how much capital you'll be trading with. Generally speaking, the higher the capital you have, the safer you'll be since you'll have more room to make mistakes.

Being undercapitalized is one of the biggest reasons' traders fail in the markets, so don't make the mistake of jumping in too soon. Also, don't try to get creative with the PDT to the detriment of your strategy. There are several gurus online who will give you 'tricks' and 'hacks' to get by this but resist the temptation.

Lastly, I've mentioned this in passing before but don't be the person who rings up their broker for investment advice. I mean, even Hollywood has figured out that this is a bad idea and has innumerable movies for you to learn from.

Your approach to trading determines how well you'll manage your risk. The real key to trading success is risk management and the simple math that underlines it. We'll look at this next.

Chapter 4 Platforms and Tools for Options Trading

A vital aspect of options trading is the platform that one uses to trade. This is because options trading requires monitoring and requires a continuous analysis of trends. Performance is also monitored, and since the trade is impacted upon by a complex of factors, one has to choose a suitable platform for trading.

A good platform for trading should offer a lot of opportunities for traders. These are opportunities to orient beginners into trading, development for the existing ones, and actualization for those with a record on the platform. A platform of trading should also prescribe the available products and any resources that subscribers on the platform can benefit from to push themselves to profitability.

With the technology developing at high speed, platforms continue to improve by the day. This is both complicating the trading itself as well as providing avenues of spreading awareness about the business. A platform should, therefore, have the ability to offer the best possible experience for the traders to do trade and grow both in experience and returns without meeting a lot of platform limitations and frustrations.

A Platform Takes Trading To the Holders

Trading involves a lot of complexities that may sometimes be scary. It makes people lose interest as soon as they develop it. They perceive it as too complicated. The impression is that it is a venture meant for the people who have higher comprehension of concepts in the economics specialty and that those who do not a background in this area will have difficulty getting on board.

However, a trading platform has to present options trading as a venture that is possible and in which anyone with interest can succeed in. The days when options trading and any other forms of trading were presented as a show of sophistication are long gone. In this era, every sector of investment is being portrayed as possible, and businesses are now being made easier in order to create a better chance for people to dare. A platform that limits investment so much and is exclusive in terms of how it carries out its trading activities is irrelevant to modern economic patterns.

Platforms, therefore, have to be interactive and user-friendly. They should have the ability to encourage users to feel like they can handle the trade. It should also have the capability to gauge the level of use and give feedback about how well they are able to use it. If it is a website, for instance, it has to be able to report the numbers as people visit it and how many eventually end up creating accounts and trading. Counting traffic is essential for feedback that can lead to the creation of a better experience for the users.

Competition

The reason for considering a good platform is because the competition is high today. Competition has led to the creation of better trading experiences through innovation. Platforms are now trying to out-do each other in being the avenues of options trading. They are doing this by striving to create ways of improving user experience. It is therefore essential to identify the various parameters of comparing the platforms. Eventually, one has to choose a platform that offers optimal access to the trading world.

In choosing a platform sometimes, one would want to take advantage of the advantages of different platforms. This is looking at one's style of trading and how they wish to monitor their business and see if a platform is more transparent in handling the tares or whether it offers a clear lens of controlling purchases and sells of options. This is the reason why the various platforms have to be assessed in terms of their potential. Usually, platforms are related to the tools of trading. Some of the tools of trading can be found right on the platform of trading.

When a platform of trading also has various tools of aiding trading, it ensures that one can gain a lot of benefits at one place. This makes the platform a utility platform where a person can visit for more purposes than just trading. It also makes it better. For instance, if a platform has videos that offer trading tutorials. This can make it resourceful in imparting competency in participating in the very sector that the platform operates.

To best benefit from competition, one has to understand the type of trade they want to do. This is by naming their price and gauging which platform can serve better in ensuring returns and value generation. This is in order to avoid going into trading in desperation, and one has to be patient to see if the platform can also come out and meet a trader at their point of ability and also help in trading in comfort where risk is at a minimum.

Types of Trading Platforms

There are various platforms in options trading that one could consider. There is web-based trading that utilizes the power of the search engines. This platform has many operators since the building of websites in the modern age is easy. This platform is responsible for the growth in the popularity of options trading. People can trade from anyone, open brokerage accounts, make deposits, and participate in the buying and selling of assets in the comfort of their homes.

With the presence of a lot of technological gadgets such as smartphones, tablets, and computers, web-based trading has been easy and possible. Websites can be built with additional resources for learning and tools that can be an advantage for both novice and seasoned traders. On the websites, regular updates on the market can be posted to keep traders informed about trends, patterns, and even help in analyzing price movements for the subscribers.

The web is also a good platform when it comes to filtering opportunities and options based on suitability and preference in view of the various abilities of users. They can be designed to be customizable even when the options markets are standardized.

User Friendliness

Usually, websites are good as they offer various tools that aid beginners to edge into trading options. ASX, for example, offers a variety of web-based resources that guide people in their efforts to understand trading. This includes online chats that have instant feedback as a team is dedicated to the work site for correspondence purposes. The aim of this is to offer motivation and impetus to go on with the discovery of the markets trends until one becomes a seasoned trader.

Friendliness is also in terms of the efforts that are made to create peer assistance. This is through creating groups of traders that influence each other and can learn from the vast experiences in the trading of the options. This can be a positive influence on the journey to gaining competence and help support an environment where people can relate and interact as they pursue their various financial goals.

It is important to consider the fact that some of the platforms of trading offer important tools that can be helpful in deciding on options. The tools are those that help in monitoring markets and simplify the technical analysis process for the trader. This can help one to sharpen their trading strategy to align well with the ultimate goal of trading. This depends on whether the goal of trading is to earn money in terms of profit or hedge oneself against losses on the underlying asset.

Tools to Learn

Upon mastering the various basics of trading and making the initial moves to start trading, one has to use various tools that help to indicate the advancers and decliners on the market. Greeks are some kind of metrics that those involved in options trading capitalize to ensure maximization of returns. These "Greeks" include the delta matrix that measures the correlation between price movements of the underlying asset relative to the price of the option. The tools for monitoring the movements for these parameters of trading are vital as everyone is always trading with a focus on minimizing losses while geared towards profit maximization.

The gamma is another tool that can help to predict market trends in order to do good timing for decisions on exercising rights in options. Gamma is an indicator of the rate of delta variations for the option price as compared to the asset price. This goes hand in hand with the time-decay tool that indicators the value movement, either upwards or downwards, in the period of life options. This helps to signal which options to avoid given the remaining time of the life span and the value implications thereon.

There is also the aspect of the volatility of the asset underlying a particular option trade. Some of the assets or stocks do not have inherent volatility to appreciate in value due to their nature. Assets that have high market volatility usually gain a lot on the market, and hence, the value behaves better to favor the call option trade. Products with ugh volatility and high inherent value are not suitable for the put option trade since they will occasion a loss. It is therefore important to use correct tools that aid in the analysis if the technical mechanics of the options trading business.

Tools are not just concrete things that can be manipulated. Some tools, especially in trading, are conceptual in nature. This is because they are the ones by which one can trade and aid in decision making. They sample out market forces and help in mapping out market trends for the benefit of the trader. To perceive tools as only concrete in nature is a misconception of the whole options trading venture.

Professional level platforms

There is a level in trading where one attains sophistication and attains the intuition to thrive in options trading regardless of the ways market forces seem to behave. At this level, someone needs tools that can help them edge into the horizon of complexity in trading. The platforms for this professional level exist, and they have to offer tools that are an edge above the basic level. These tools have to offer strategies of competing to control the stocks and rise above the market forces. At this level, one becomes daring, and the possibilities that the platform offers should only be dared by those who have mastered trading and are sure of beating odds as they speculate about squeezing out value form trades that otherwise be perceived as highly risky.

The platform should be full of idea probing resources that lead one to gain the courage to trade more and more. Web-based platforms of this level include the think or swim platform that is categorically for seasoned traders. This is the reason why one has to know the platform to trade on based on their level of experience in options trading. Some platforms are too complicated for the starters. The tools are even out of the capacity of a beginner to comprehend the trades appear to have higher risks that may wipe away hard-earned fortunes.

Mobile Trading

Some platforms have taken advantage of the handiness of the mobile era. These entail the smartphone lifestyle and the flashier iPod, iPad, and tablet culture. This is when trading is being placed in the palms of traders to hold and run away with it. This platform usually targets traders that want to capitalize on device optimization. This is the reason why trades have classes. Some of the options could be device targeted as they can only be taken advantage of when one using the suitable device for trading, provided the relevant support tools that the device offers.

Mobile trading also comes in order to keep people abreast. This is because opportunities sometimes appear and disappear on people because they are not using a device that enables them to be precise and timely in decision making and action.

With mobile trading, apps have been developed, some with notification capability. One can customize the apps to ensure that no opportunity comes that is not taken advantage of. Opportunities' in trading have to be seized and relying on a platform that is less handy and far means that opportunities of trading are lost.

What Are We Looking For In Platforms And Tools?

First is the opportunity to learn. There is no worse platform of trading than that which targets only to admit traders who do not understand what they are getting into. The education that a platform has to offer should be free as trading is itself risky enough to prohibit any extra expenses in the process. Platform operators should understand that any interested person who visits their platform is a potential subscriber, and they should freely offer support to educate them for the purpose of acquisition of requisite knowledge on options trading.

Some of the platforms have gone as opening structures units for education on options trading. These courses are taken online, and coaching is done through the provision of a stream of webinars transmitted live or uploading recorded ones. This is for platforms that appreciate that trading is an informed gamble that requires one to know enough. They even test the proficiency of understanding trading concepts and mechanics for the purpose of ensuring that any people who trade on the platform are doing what they understand to build the platform ratings.

It is also vital for a starter to set standards that the broker's customer service should pass. In trading, brokers should work enough to earn the commission that they charge on the options that subscribers trade on buy. This is because some brokers are obscure and may not involve the options trader who is buying options in decisions that directly impact on his capital. One, therefore, faces a lot of anxiety if the broker is not responsive and transparent on the particular mechanics that influence trade.

Excellent broker services try to suit customer needs. They ask options traders subscribed to their platform what their preferred means of reaching is. Whether a live chat or phone call suits the customer or not. They also dedicate a desk for trading communications and queries and has the discipline to listen to customers and their issues with patience. They, in fact, have feedback on the quality of customer service that those who reach out get.

Software Trading Platforms

These are more complex than web-based ones. This is because they are run on the trader's computer, and the trader is required to understand what the software does and interpret it. Even when the brokerage can offer assistance, software-based platforms require the trader to have enough technical know how to read charts, graphs, and understand patterns that represent various components of options trading.

For beginners, a complex platform has to be avoided by all means. This is because one is bound to engage in aspects of trading that they do not have an understanding of. A trading platform simply has to be simple and clear. The interface should not be too busy as to scare away those traders who are not accustomed. This is the reason why operators usually separate the platforms that as designed for basic use, which is suitable for novices, and advanced trading for the seasoned ones.

Then a broker has to offer a tutorial that guides the user on how to navigate their platform. Everything has to be explained, even those that one would deem to be obvious. Screenshots can even be available in order to be categorical and emphatic. This ensures that a broker has offered all possible assists for the trader to benefit from the offers and products on the platform successfully.

Cost Implication

It is important for the trader to know that some brokers may have charges attached to some of the services, resources, and tools that they provide on their platform. These have to be assessed in terms of their worth and whether the costs are necessary. Making some tolls premium may be an indicator of quality but not always. This is particularly the case when other platforms provide similar services toll-free. Screening tools are particularly the ones that are bound to attract charges because they have abilities to analyze and assess market trends. They can do the thinking for the trader and help him in decision making. One has to read about the specifications of the tools and ascertain what they or cannot do. This is in order to know if they are customizable for the purpose of serving the needs and conveniences of traders.

Some charges can even be attached to the quotes update feed. Usually, the quotes can be accessed in real time for those who want to see them in real time. The quotes are important in influencing idea generation and sometimes can tip people of opportunities in the market. There is usually a delay for those who access the quotes updates for free.

It is also vital to understand platforms do not provide all the tools to everyone using their platform to trade. Some of the cutting-edge tools that can best serve the business interests of traders are premium. They have subscription charges or otherwise only appear on the accounts of traders who constantly sustain a certain threshold of account balance minimums. This is particularly the case for platforms that operate at the professional level. They require one to be active and remain active in trading since this serves the business interests of the brokerage through the commissions it earns on options contracts. In return, it offers the consultancy, expertise, and resource repository for one to realize value out of the options trades. This is why they attach a price on some of the tools.

One can only trust a platform that has a reputation for efficiency. This is a platform that ensures orders have a quick span of execution. This particularly for traders who understand the benefits of entering quick and instantly exiting from offered positions. The charges of platform subscription also matter. This is whether they are monthly or per year. It is vital to understand the way of earning waivers on platform fees. It could be through ensuring compliance with balance minimums or activity of trades per a set span of time.

6	2.930		27,000	2.180		4.500	0.000	شركة غيران أبوظبي
0	2.160		1,225	5.350	5.690	0.450	0.000	بنك الشرق
0	5.340		0	0.000	0.410	564,494	2.600	0.000	شركة أبوظبي الوطنية للتأمين
0	0.450		30,393	2.440	2.750	92,464	1.600	0.000	شركة العالمية القابضة
0	2.600		5,000	1.600	1.830	56,512	2.290	0.000	شركة أبوظبي الوطنية للفنادق
0	1.600		73,778	2.300	2.310	128,544	3.090	0.000	أسمنت
0				0.000	3.100	874,820	2.950	0.000	
						0	1.450		

Chapter 5   Basic Investment Strategies

Everyone who wants to avoid being broke or living from payslip to payslip has to have the right investment strategy. An investment strategy is a plan for making the money you already have given birth or multiply to more money.

Two Investment Factors to Consider When Choosing an Investment

Therefore, good investments have to have liquidity, meaning that whatever you invest in has to be easily convertible into cash at hand. Investments are risky, though, meaning that it's not guaranteed to get your intended profits always because, at any time, your investments can devalue. It is, therefore, essential to carefully examine your investments and see how much it's likely to yield; this is called looking at the potential returns. Looking through all these possibilities will help a person determine what type of investment to go for.

An investment strategy is best if it works to meet your needs. You should not go for investment only because it's trending; it may not work for you. Going for what works for you will ensure that you stick to your investment for long and that you are swayed away by other trends. The best way to find an investment that works for you is by getting something that defines you, and that would be something you're patient about.

It is good for young people to take more risks in investments by going for high growing stock investments. While for someone who is about to go into retirement, it's essential that they take fewer risks and distribute their assets to bonds.

Security Type

A security type is the kind of investment you hold, and it should always be diverse.

Cash and Bank Security

This type has very high liquidity because you are dealing with cash at hand that you take to the bank at any time and also withdraw at will. It has low risk because unless you need the money, it is safely kept at the bank. But this, however, means that it has no potential for growth and can even lose its value in case there is inflation. The biggest advantage with this, however, is that you have access at any needed time. Banks also offer emergency funds, and therefore in case you urgently need money, you do not have to wait for long.

Certificate of Deposit

The liquidity in this is low because you cannot withdraw cash whenever you want. You can only get the money after the agreed time with the bank. The risk is low because the money is safely kept at the bank. However, it's potential for growth is very minimal since it has a specified rate of interest. This means that your money is lying in a bank waiting for a certain interest rate instead of taking chances elsewhere. The growth rate is so low and not worth the time you waited to get the interest.

Stocks

Whenever people think about investments, they think stock. The liquidity is high because you get to buy shares from a company and share their profits. You can purchase shares from one or as many companies as you can and therefore get to enjoy a certain percentage of their earnings. The risk is medium because as much as you enjoy the profits, you are also involved with their losses. Therefore, this means that you should not expect to be paid when the company you have shared with is not making profits. However, all investments go through this uncertainty; there is no single investment that won't have a loss risk. The potential for growth in this is very high as you get to grow, the more the company grows. Every company's objective is to yield profits, and therefore companies will continue putting their best foot forward to make sure they do not incur losses. The more they work on this, the more their profits. The more the company's profits, the more your shares, therefore, the reason why the potential growth is high.

Bonds

The liquidity in this is medium because it involves you getting to give some of your money as a loan to a company or government. Then after the agreed time, your money is returned to you along with the interest you agreed on. The interest rates may be very high or low, depending on who you have loaned. If you lend big companies or treasury, you are much secured, and therefore the returns in this are small. The risk comes in because you may give loans to what is known as junk bonds, and you risk not being paid or having partial payments. However, since junk bonds do not guarantee security, they make sure to offer a little higher return than large corporate that guarantees security. The potential for growth is medium because it depends if you are paid and the profits you make from the payments.

Real Estate

The liquidity is low because it involves lands and buildings. Converting lands and buildings is dependent on the value the assets have accumulated over time. This is because if you need to have cash from these investments, then you have to make sure you are selling at a better price than you used when buying them. This makes the risk medium because they are assets and may either maintain their value or grow. If they don't grow, it is a disadvantage to the investor, but if the assets grow in value, then the investor has made it. Potential for growth is medium because of how long it takes to generate value finally.

Precious Metals

The liquidity is very high because it involves buying of precious metals like gold and silver. When you buy precious metals, you can easily convert them into cash by selling them at an even higher price than you bought it. The risk is medium because the metals need a lot of proper handling to ensure that they do spoil, and also most buyers tend to buy at very low prices. The potential growth is medium because it depends on the available market and the demand as well.

Derivatives

The liquidity is medium. You can either convert your earnings quickly, depending on how accessible the stocks you bought are. Here you get to purchase stocks from another stock instead of making a direct purchase. And for this to happen, you have to believe that the stock you are buying from will increase its value. The risk is very high because you depend on another stock to earn your profits without being directly involved. If the stock does not allow you to buy in a more valuable stock, then you are unlikely to make any value out of it. The potential for growth, however, is very high since you only get to buy from stocks that have value.

It is important to be diverse in your investments; this means that you do not settle on a particular type. If you are able to split your assets, you are in a better secure position. When there is a downfall in one sector, you can count on another industry. But if you hold all your assets in one industry and the sector goes down, you will significantly suffer as an investor because you will lose everything. Something else worth noting is that one should be careful with their investment as they get older. One mistake from such a person can lead them into a very desperate life after retirement.

Investing Strategies

Buy and Hold

This calls for thorough research before entirely going into any investment. After the research, you should settle for a long term investment of like ten years. You should then buy this investment and hold it irrespective of how many temptations that you may come through along the way to sell them. Sometimes it may be so tempting to sell it because the price at which you are being offered is a little tempting, but you should be able to resist. An investor should only sell if the rules for sticking to the stock are no longer favorable. This may happen in that either there is a sign that the stocks are no longer maintainable. This could be from the fact that the company is taking a different strategy than what you signed up for, and there you get uncomfortable to continue. You may also sell only. if you have had enough before the end of the long-term, and you want to opt-out. It should never be out of greed, thinking that what you are being offered is too good to resist because you do not know how much better you are likely to get. There is, however, a downside to this, as explained below. You may do great research and have everything correctly figured out. You may yield your investments after the long-term you had invested in. However, when retirement sinks in, you need the money urgently because that's your only survival hope. The other downside is that you may have made the wrong choice all along. Then with buy and hold strategy, you may make a lot of loss that will kick you out of the market even if unwilling to.

This type of investment is often referred to as time in the market strategy because of how investors wait until very long to avoid short term dangers. This then means that the investor does not have to keep on trading like in other strategies because they are doing it for the long-term. This strategy is the opposite of the absolute market timing strategy. The absolute market timing strategy believes that an investor should transact within short-term periods. There, an investor in the absolute market will buy and sell within small durations aiming to purchase at low prices but eventually selling at very high prices.

Several portfolios use the buy and hold strategy. They are, however, often known as the lazy portfolios. These are some of those portfolios.

Portfolios under the buy and hold strategy.

- Core and satellite – this is a time tested investment that has a core, which is the big capital, which has the most significant investment; it also has other smaller investments. This is done so that the investments are spread out in order to achieve very big returns with very low risks.
- Modern portfolio theory- This means that the investor does all he can to have very low risks in the market, while still yielding very high returns in any given portfolio of his investments. In short, what the investor does in this is that he holds one given asset, mutual fund, and security each at a time. The individual types are usually highly risky, but when they are put together with other many types, they get a balance. The balance created ensures that the risk is lower than the primary assets.

- Postmodern portfolio theory- the difference between this and modern portfolio theory is how the two view risks. The modern portfolio views risks as having several different types of investments that have many risk stages come together in order to yield significant returns. It actually focuses on risks and returns. On the other hand, a post-modern portfolio investor focuses on the behavior instead of settling on the calculations aspect the way a modern portfolio investor does.
- Tactical asset allocation – This is where an investor gets to put together all the different strategies. The investor in this will work out to ensure that stocks, bonds, and cash balance so that he gets more significant profits at low risks by comparing the index. The tactical asset allocation investment strategy differs from technical analysis and fundamental analysis in that it focuses on assets rather than on the type of investment to select.

Value Investment

This means that you go for stocks that are more underestimated than the other stocks. In short, it means going for stocks that most people are unlikely to go for. This is risky but brave because you are not following the crowd. In doing this, you go for companies that are just beginning to grow and have not attracted the big fish in the market; you can also go for companies that were only recently established. You can stick to this investment until you feel that you are doing quite well or have achieved more than you expected before eventually selling. This, however, does not come without a possible risk, as explained below.

Being an active trader makes you have easy, quick access to more significant returns. However, that also means that as quick as it is to make profits, it's also very easy and fast to make losses. Therefore, it is usually recommended that you use small investments instead of putting in too much for this kind of trading because anything can happen. It is better to lose small than to lose hugely, and therefore, not taking the risk is very important.

Fundamental Analysis

In this strategy, you analyze financial statements so that you are able to choose the best stock for you as an investor. What happens is that there is a data comparison of the financial statements of all the current and past data, for all the business within the industry which you intend to venture. This helps determine the total price of the stock and also determines if the stock is really worth the purchase.

Technical Analysis

In this, technical traders use charts that help them observe the price patterns in the present, and all the trends are happening within the market. When they observe this, they are then able to foretell what may happen in the future for these markets. From technical analysis, signals, indicators, and patterns are very important because they determine the future of the trade. These are essential for the investor because they help him make decisions based on whatever signal they give. The signals may warn that it is time to buy or sell or even stop a trade. An investor has to obey because they solely depend on these unavoidable patterns.

Growth Investing

This means going for stocks in well-established companies; companies are already doing well and attracting a lot of potential. This means that everyone is already running for these investments, and they are doing pretty well. There is even evidence of how well the companies are doing. People investing in this have a lot of faith in this investment because they expect that it only keeps growing. People buying in this type of investment do not mind buying at a high price because they know that they will sell even bigger than they bought it. Therefore, what happens here is that you go for big and well-known companies. These are companies that are well known and have been in the market for long.

The right investment strategy, however, still goes back to an individual. What works for an investor is very important instead of relying on what worked for others. It may have worked for others but not work for you. It is good, however, to involve all the strategies as you make decisions as an individual investor.

Chapter 6   How Options Are Priced

Understanding Strike Price

A strike price is a fixed price at which an options contract can be exercised. The term is mainly used when describing index and stock options.

How strike price works

The options contract has specified stripe prices. In put options, the value of the underlying asset while trading is referred to as the strike price. In call options, the holder earns the right to buy an underlying asset at the set strike price up to the expiry date. In put options, it is the price the underlying asset is traded by an option buyer up to the expiry date. In the call option, the strike price refers to the amount an investor buys the underlying asset up to the expiry date. The strike price is also referred to as the exercise price. It is an essential factor in establishing the value of an option.

Importance of Strike Price

While pricing options, this is the most crucial factor to consider. While exercising an option, the profit earned is determined by the difference between the stock's market price and the option strike price at the expiration date. A strike price can help you establish if an investment is worth your time or not. You can come out with a loss or a profit depending on the strike price involved. As an investor, you want to know the investments that bring high returns and avoid those that will result in a loss. Knowing the strike price can help you deciding on which trades to make. You also get to avoid the trades that could result in losing your investment.

The Concept of Moneyness

Moneyness refers to the quality of a financial contract. This occurs if the contract settlement is financial. It can be established by obtaining the difference between the strike price and the current trade price for an underlying asset.

Terms like out-of-the-money, in-the-money, and at-the-money can be used to explain the moneyness of options in trading.

Intrinsic Value

The intrinsic value can also be referred to as the monetary value of an asset. It is the quality of an underlying asset if it is exercised immediately. A call can get a positive intrinsic value if the stock price of the underlying asset is higher than the set price, which is the strike price. This is what we refer to as in-the-money. Out-of-the-money occurs when a put option has no value.

Time Value

This refers to the value of an option, excluding the intrinsic value. It occurs when it is difficult to establish the future price movements of an asset. Knowing the time value can aid in establishing the possible discounts that are in an option between when it was bought and when it expires. The time value is negative when it comes to European options. This is influenced by the fact that the option cannot be exercised until it gets to the expiration date.

Why Should You Care About How Options Are Priced?

As an investor, it is very crucial to know how various options are priced. Knowing the prices saves one from the possibility of being overpriced or underpriced depending on the situation at hand. While evaluating the prices, you also get to identify the possible investments that you can engage in depending on your budget. This, alongside other reasons, shows the importance of knowing how options are priced. Below I have discussed a number of reasons why it's important that you have an understanding of the options trading pricing.

1. It allows you to know what to invest in.

As a beginner, you may be stranded and unable to identify the best investment that you can engage in. Before engaging in a trade, it is always good to conduct a proper evaluation. This analysis helps you know all that is required if you before engaging in business. Understanding the prices helps you know that which you can afford to invest in. You will find that some options demand that you spend a vast some money. While at it, you will identify some that need little investments.

The one that demands that you part with a small portion of your finances may appear to be very appealing. You will find that most amateur trades will prefer beginning with such. After all, you get to the part with a small piece of your income and generate profits. You forget to put all other factors into consideration, such as option strategies and end up focusing on the price. Higher chances are that you are likely to encounter a massive loss in the trade since you know very little about what you are engaging in. This is why you should consider the pricing before engaging in any form of commerce.

While getting a brokerage account, you need to be very careful with the features and services provided by the account. By evaluating the option pricing, you will identify accounts that have peculiar pricing, and this should raise the alarm. The pricing that does not rhyme with the rest should help you know the official brokerage accounts and those that are not genuine. As the options trading markets expand, we have a lot of competition being created. This results in the creations on multiple accounts of which, some are a pure scam. Knowing the options pricing will help you identify the excellent option trading accounts.

In some cases, you may find some trades that have high pricing. You also find that the returns are equally good, and it appears like an excellent investment to make. When you decide to engage in it, you may end up getting a considerable profit. If at all, you had no information about the option and especially the pricing, it would be challenging to execute it. The fact that you have knowledge of the pricing helps you identify it as a good investment, and you decide to engage in the trade.

2. You can identify the best option strategy to use. You find that each procedure is different in its ways, and the pricing varies. Knowing option pricing will help you identify the best strategy to utilize in every situation. While analyzing the various Options strategies, you may discover that some are more profitable than others. In some cases, one may not get any profit and remain at a stagnant point without making returns. This information becomes useful in that it guides you in investing in the right strategy.

3.   You can minimize risks

It is expected that the investment in options trading comes with its risks. There are a number of challenges that you will encounter. On the bright side, some of these downsides can be predicted. Due to this factor, it becomes easy to manage them and make the right trade. If you can look into option pricing, managing some of these risks becomes easy. You can evaluate the option pricing and get to know the trades that are not profitable. Imagine the amount of trouble you will have saved yourself from if you knew how the options are priced.

4.   There is room for increasing return

The dream of every investor is to get the highest possible profits. You want to see yourself running a profitable business that will unbelievably transform your income generation ability. This does not only have to be a dream, but you can make it happen. Knowing how options are priced enables you to establish the options that are profitable. Trading in such opportunities will help you earn high returns and make your dreams a reality.

5.   It helps in choosing a cost-effective option

We are regularly advised to live within our means. I am a believer that people should also trade within their means. While deciding on the best option to invest in, try to aim at choosing a cost-effective strategy. By doing so, you will be able to trade in that which you can afford. If things go contrary to what you anticipated, you will get a loss, but it will not be as bad as if never invested in what you can afford to lose. The option prices play a significant role in having a cost-effective option.

From the above reasons provided, it is clear why you need to be concerned about how options are priced. The option pricing has a significant influence on options trading. It helps you identify the best options to engage in. If you have a vision of becoming an expert in options trading, you should be able to take a close look into the option pricing. You will identify the options that can result in a loss and those that are profitable and worth investing your income on. To make a fortune out of your investment, consider taking a keen look at how options are priced.

Key Influencers of Options Prices

The only way to determine the price value if an option is to establish what contributes to its value. Things are priced differently depending on their value. When you intend to purchase a car, you have probably thought of the model you intend to get. What makes a Lamborghini more expensive than a Toyota? Well, the price narrows down to the quality of the car. This applies to almost every other commodity that can be sold. The quality is usually the core determining factor while coming up with the price. When it comes to investing, the price value will discover the income you are likely to generate. If you aspire to trade in a successful venture, you may be required to use a large portion of your income equally. This is because the high quality of goods and services are highly-priced. The vice versa is also applicable. The low-priced commodities that low quality and are likely to result in a small income-generating investment. The prices will tell you a lot about the investment you choose to undertake. Below are the key influencing factors while pricing options.

The Type of Options

We have two types of options: a call option, and a put option. This is the basis in establishing the price of an item. Depending on the fact the type of option involved, the costs will differ. In a call option, the investor earns the right to purchase the underlying asset at an agreed-upon duration at the set price. In a put option, the investor has the right to trade the underlying instrument at a set price within the specified period. In a situation whereby you have the long a call or are short a put, the value of the option goes high as the market value increases. When you are short a call or long a put, the option value will increase as the market value declines.

Stock Price

This is the value of a stock. In some situations, the call option may permit you to purchase a stock at an agreed-upon price. The cost of the capital may rise in the future, resulting in the option being worth more than it already is. The same applies if the prices lack the potential to increase, this will mean that the value of the stock will go low, and as a result, you encounter a loss. For instance, you may buy the stock at $ 200 and maybe shortly it has the potential of rising to $ 220. another person may obtain a share at $ 100 and in the near future, the value of the stock decreases to $ 70. You will end up with a loss of $ 30. Ideally, one would instead go with the capital that has the probability of increasing in the future. This way, you will end up making a profit as opposed to ending up with a loss in your investment.

Strike Price

The strike price operates the same as the stock price. A strike price refers to the fixed amount of money in which a derivative contract can be exercised or bought. While dealing with stocks, this is a term that you will come across severally. In a put option, the strike price refers to the amount that the underlying asset is traded by the option buyer while at the expiry date. In a call option, the strike price refers to the price the underlying asset can be purchased by the option buyer up to the expiry. The rates will differ depending on the type of strike price.

The Expiration Date

You have heard of some contracts being regarded as worthless upon getting to the expiry date. The reason behind it is since their value is no longer in existence once the contract expires. The expiration date in options trading refers to the duration in which an option contract is of importance and after which it is considered valueless. You find that the expiry date greatly influences the option prices, and if you are not keen, you may end up making a loss.

This means that the best time to buy or sell options when the cost is high, that is any period before the expiry date is. You find that beginners are at times deceived and sold for an option that is almost becoming worthless and as a result, end up making losses.

Interest Rates

The interest rates do not have a massive impact on the option value, but they have minimal influence. The amount of a call option rises when there is an increase in interest rates, and the value of the put option falls. Alternatively, when the interest rates decline the value of the call option will also become lower, and the put options will rise. The second option becomes attractive when the interest rates increase. In a situation where the interest goes up, you will be able to earn more. This shows how interest rates influence prices.

Volatility

In determining the option prices, we use forward volatility. Forward volatility refers to the quantity of implied volatility during the duration in the future. The implied volatility refers to the implied movement of stocks. It acts as an indicator of the direction the stock moves. Some moves result from increases in the value of the capital. Also, some moves result from declining in the amount of money. When the stock value lowers its prices also decrease. In an event, the stock value increases the prices are also bound to increase. This is how the volatility influences the rates.

Dividends

A dividend refers to the regular total payment made by a company to its shareholders. It results from the profits made by a company. In most cases, options do not get dividends. If bonuses are given out, the option value will fluctuate. An ex-dividend date is provided once a company gives out profits. Dividends can be given out if you have stocks at the time of their release. When this occurs, it also influences the value of the capital, causing it to decrease with the number of dividends. The call value lowers, and the put value goes above in a situation whereby the bonuses increase. This is how profits influence the prices of options.

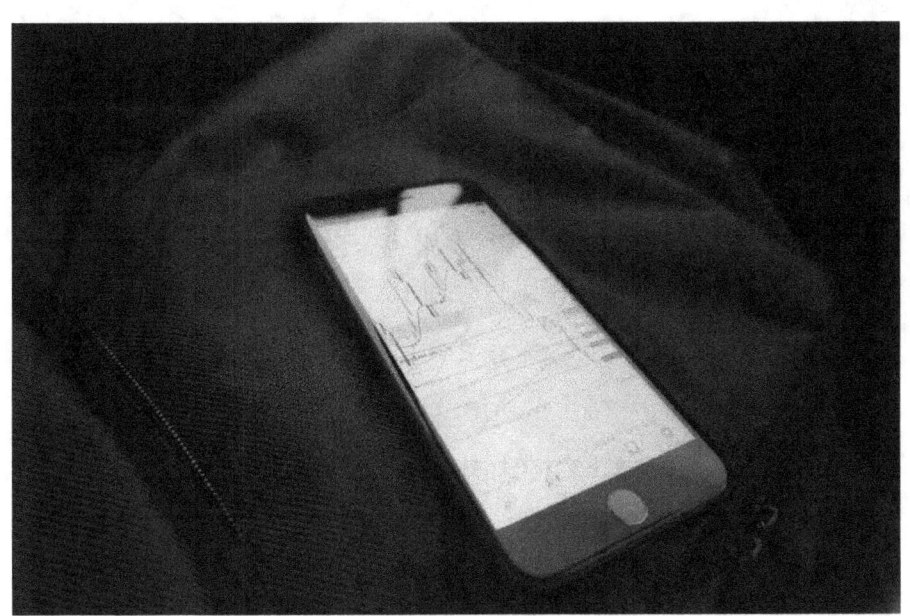

Chapter 7 Risk Management

Excellent risk management can save the worst trading strategy, but horrible risk management will sink even the best strategy. This is a lesson that many traders learn painfully over time, and I suggest you learn this by heart and install it deep within you even if you can't fully comprehend that statement.

Risk management has many different elements to both quantitative and qualitative. When it comes to options trading, the quantitative side is minimal thanks to the nature of options limiting risk by themselves. However, the qualitative side deserves a lot of attention. This chapter is going to give you the risk management framework that you need to succeed.

Risk

So what is risk anyway? Logically, it is the probability of you losing all of your money. In trading terms, you can think of it as being the probability of your actions putting you on a path to losing all of your capital. A good way to think about the need for good risk management is to ask yourself what a bad trader would do? Forget trading, what would a bad business person do with their capital?

Well, they would spend it on useless stuff that adds nothing to the bottom line. They would also increase expenses, market poorly, not take care of their employees, and be indisciplined with regards to their processes. While trading, you don't have employees or marketing needs, so you don't need to worry about that.

Do you have suppliers and costs? Well, yes, you do. Your supplier is your broker, and you pay fees to execute your trades. That is the cost of access. In directional trading, you have high costs as well because taking losses is a necessary part of trading. With market neutral or non-directional trading, your losses are going to be minimal, but you should still seek to minimize them.

What about discipline? Do you think you can trade and analyze the market well if you've just returned home from your job and are tired? If you didn't sleep properly last night? Or if you've argued with your spouse or partner? The point I'm making is that the more you behave like a terrible business owner, the more you increase your risk of failure.

Odds and Averages

Trading requires you to think a bit differently about profitability. In the previous paragraphs, I spoke about minimizing costs, and your first thought must have been to seek to reduce losses and maximize wins. This is a natural product of linear or ordered thinking. The market, however, is chaotic and linear thinking is going to get you nowhere.

Instead, you need to think in terms of averages and odds. Averages imply that you need to worry about your average loss size and your average win size. Seek to decrease the former and increase the latter. Notice that when we talk about averages, we're not necessarily talking about reducing the total number of losses. You can reduce the average by either reducing the sum of your losses or by increasing the number of losing trades while keeping the sum of the losses constant. This is a shift in thinking you must make.

Thinking in this way sets you up nicely to think in terms of odds, because in chaotic systems all you can bank on are odds playing out in the long run. For example, if you flip a coin, do you know in advance whether it's going to be a heads or tails? Probably not. But if someone asked you to predict the distribution of heads versus tails over 10,000 flips, you could reasonably guess that it'll be 5000 heads and 5000 tails. You might be off by a few flips either way, but you'll be pretty close percentage-wise.

In fact, the greater the number of flips, the lesser your error percentage. This is because the odds inherent in a pattern that occurs in a chaotic system express themselves best over the long run. Your trading strategy is precisely such a pattern. The market is a chaotic system. Hence, you should focus on executing your strategy as it is meant to be executed over and over again and worry about profitability only in the long run.

Contrast this with the usual attitude of traders who seek to win every single trade. This is impossible to accomplish since no trading strategy or pattern is correct 100% of the time. If we were discussing directional strategies, I'd spend a lot more time on this, but the fact is that options take care of a lot of this ambiguity themselves.

This is because you don't have to do much when trading options. You enter and then monitor the trade. Sure, it helps to have some directional bias, but even if you get it wrong, your losses will be extremely limited, and you're more likely to hit winners than losers.

Despite this, always think of your strategy in terms of its odds. There are two basic metrics to measure this. The first is the win rate of your system. This is simply the percentage of winners you have. The second is your payout ratio which is the average win size divided by the average loss size.

Together these two metrics will determine how profitable your system is. Both of them play off one another, and an increase in one is usually met by a decrease in another. It takes an extremely skillful trader to increase both simultaneously.

Risk Per Trade

The quantitative side of risk management when it comes to options trading is lesser than what you need to take care of when trading directionally. However, this doesn't mean there's nothing to worry about. Perhaps the most important metric of them all is your risk per trade. The risk per trade is what ultimately governs your profitability.

How much should you risk per trade? Common wisdom says that you should restrict this to 2% of your capital. For options trading purposes, this is perfectly fine. In fact, once you build your skill and can see opportunities better, I'd suggest increasing it to a higher level.

A point that you must understand here is that you must keep your risk per trade consistent for it to have any effect. You might see a wonderful setup and think that it has no chance of failure, but the truth is that you don't know how things will turn out. Even the prettiest setup has every chance of failing, and the ugliest setup you can think of may result in a profit. So never adjust your position size based on how something looks.

Calculating your position size for a trade is a pretty straightforward task. Every option's strategy will have a fixed maximum risk amount. Divide the capital risk by this amount, and that gives you your position size. Round that down to the nearest whole number since you can only buy whole number lots when it comes to contract sizes.

For example, let's say your maximum risk is $50 per lot on the trade. Your capital is $10,000. Your risk per trade is 2%. So the amount you're risking on that trade is 2% of 10,000 which is $200. Divide this by 50, and you get 4. Hence, your position size is four contracts or 400 shares. (You'll buy the contracts, not the shares.)

Why is it important to keep your risk per trade consistent? Well, recall that your average win and loss size is important when it comes to determining your profitability. These, in conjunction with your strategy's success rate, determine how much money you'll make. If you keep shifting your risk amount per trade, you'll shift your win and loss sizes. You might argue that since it's an average, you can always adjust amounts to reflect an average.

My counter to that is how would you know which trades to adjust in advance? You won't know which ones are going to be a win or a loss, so you won't know which trade sizes to adjust to meet the average. Hence, keep it consistent across all trades and let the math work for you.

Aside from risk per trade, there are some simple metrics you should keep track of as part of your quantitative risk management plan.

Drawdown

A drawdown refers to the reduction in capital your account experiences. Drawdowns by themselves always occur. The metrics you should be measuring are the maximum drawdown and recovery period. If you think of your account's balance as a curve, the maximum drawdown is the biggest peak to trough distance in dollars. The recovery period is the subsequent time it took for your account to make new equity high.

If your risk per trade is far too high, your max drawdown will be unacceptably high. For example, if you risk 10% per trade and lose two in a row, which is very likely, your drawdown is going to be 20%. This is an absurdly large hole to dig your way out. Consider that your capital has decreased by 20% and the subsequent climb back up needs to be done on lesser capital than previously.

This is why you need to keep your risk per trade low and in line with your strategy's success rate. The best way to manage drawdowns and limit the damage they cause is to put in place risk limits per day, week, and month. Even professional athletes who train to do one thing all the time have bad days, so it's unfair to expect yourself to be at 100% all the time.

These risk limits will take you out of the game when you're playing poorly. A daily risk limit is to prevent you from getting into a spiral of revenge trading. A good limit to stick to when starting off is to stop trading if you experience three losses in a row. This is pretty unlikely with options trades to be honest unless you screw up badly, but it's good to have a limit in place from a perspective of discipline.

Next, aim for a maximum weekly drawdown limit of 5% and a monthly drawdown limit of 6-8%. These are pretty high limits, to be honest, and if you are a directional trader, these limits do not apply to you. Directional traders need to be a lot more conservative than options trader when it comes to risk.

Understand that these are hard stop limits. So if your account has hit its monthly drawdown level within the first week, you need to take the rest of the month off. Overtrading and a lack of reflection on progress can cause a lot of damage, and a drawdown is simply a reflection of that.

Qualitative Risk

Quantitative metrics aside, your ability to properly manage qualitative things in your life and trading will dictate a lot of your success. Prepare well, and you're likely to see progress. You need to see preparation as your responsibility. I mean, no one else can prepare for you can they?

There are different elements to tracking your level of preparation so let's look at them one by one.

Health

You can't trade if you're physically unfit. If you have a fever or if you're suffering from some condition that makes it impossible for you to concentrate, forget about trading. You can rest assured that the other traders in the market will be more than happy to take your money.

When viewed from an options trading perspective, the risk is even more acute. All options strategies will require you to write options at some point, even the most basic ones like in this book. Even if your position is covered, making a mistake, and having an option you wrote be exercised by the buyer is an unpleasant thing that happens. Maintain a regimen of exercise and eat healthy food. Depending on how long you sit in front of your screen, you might even want to consider avoiding certain foods when in session.

Heavy meals and food that makes you drowsy will cause your performance to dip, so avoid eating them when you're in the market. Also, don't exercise to such an extent that you're completely exhausted. The idea is to be fresh and alert, not fatigued and aching for a good sleep.

You might have an image of traders as being highly wired and as people who spend their entire lives in front of a screen. Well, most traders do sit in front of a screen most of the time, but the successful ones make time for other stuff in their lives as well. So don't try to copy some false vision here. Instead, do what feels comfortable to you while taking care to not slip into habits that are detrimental to your success.

Lifestyle

Your fitness is just one part of your lifestyle, of course. Is your lifestyle conducive to profitable trading? Are you someone who loves staying up at all sorts of odd hours and considers it perfectly normal to stumble onto a work task while hungover or worse? Make no mistake, the market will make you donate all of your capital to it.

Many beginners underestimate how difficult trading is. This should come as no surprise since beginners by definition underestimate anything. What shocks most of them is the degree to which they underestimate the difficulty of trading successfully. Let me put it in writing for you: Trading is one of the most challenging things you will ever do in your life.

The reason it is so difficult is due to the ever-changing nature of the market and the mental demands it places upon you. Another key lifestyle question to consider is the hours when you'll trade. Most of you reading this probably have full-time jobs and cannot spend your whole day in front of the market.

So plan out when you'll trade and how you'll prepare yourself for the session. What routines will you carry out? If you're going to trade in the morning before work begins, how will you manage to do this? Will you work in a quiet place or in some noisy truck stop on the way to work? Options positions don't need a lot of maintenance, so there's not much need for this, but when will you check in on the market throughout the day? Will you check in a few times? Five times? Define everything to do with your routine.

Think of yourself as a professional athlete who has to show up for a game everyday. An athlete has a precise method of preparation before showing up for a game. They don't deviate from their preparatory routine and certainly don't experiment with new things during game time. Practice is when they try out new stuff.

How will you practice your skills and improve your ability to execute your strategy? When will you do this? Plan it all out and develop your success routine.

Mental States

Trading is a mental activity. You don't need to lift or push anything physically. Therefore it is crucial to ensure that your mental state is as optimal as it needs to be for you to execute properly. Having a checklist or a mental check-in list works wonders for the trading process.

Before any trading, write down what's going through your mind and ask yourself how you feel. If you find that you're tired or frustrated and unable to focus properly, step away, and do not trade. If you're planning on sitting in front of your terminal for more than an hour, make it a habit to check in with yourself every half hour or hourly. This need not be a detailed examination, just a simple check-in with yourself to see how things are going.

Take your risk management tasks seriously, and the market will reward you with profits. Do not be the trader who stumbles into the market completely unprepared and then wonders why trading is so unforgiving. Above all else, seek to eliminate all sources of stress when it comes to trading. Take regular breaks and schedule months off from the market to recap and assimilate the things you've learned and need to improve.

Trading every single day of the year does not make sense. This isn't a job where you'll be rewarded with a certain salary for just showing up. You need to produce results, and in order to do so, you need to manage your downside carefully.

An excellent practice is to actually review how you work and set aside months exclusively for trading and months exclusively for practice purposes. By practice, I mean reviewing your prior results, working on your mindset and improving your risk management abilities. This is an unconventional method of working but it will pay massive dividends down the line.

Now that you have a better understanding of the basics, it's finally time to jump in and take a look at various trading strategies you can deploy with options.

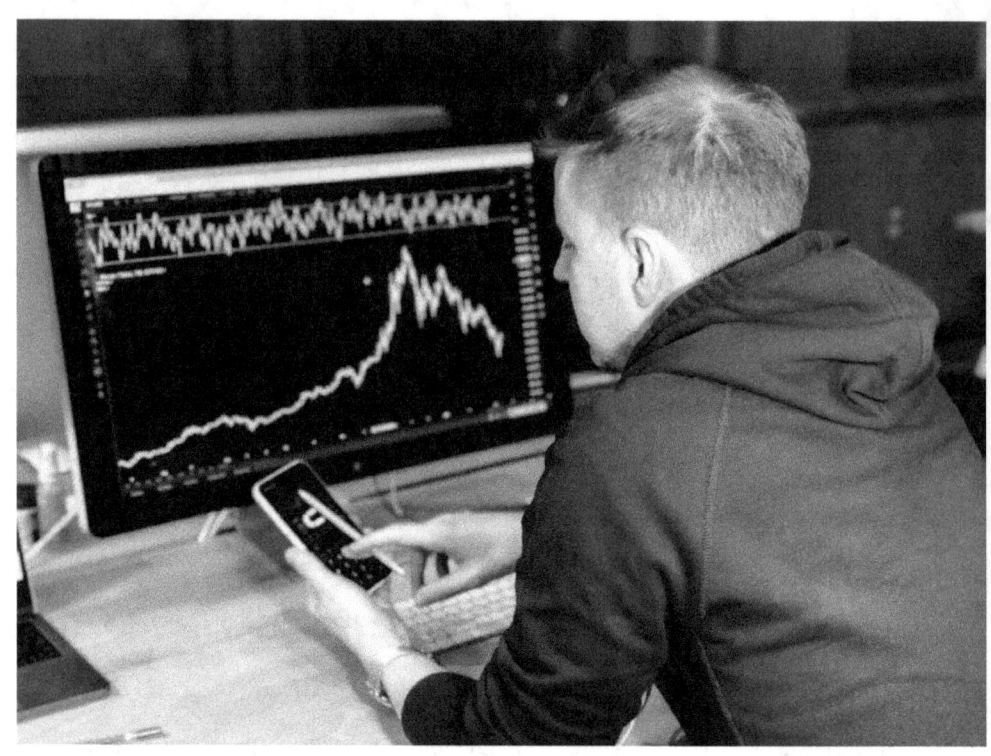

Chapter 8
The Basics Of Technical Analysis

Technical analysis is the method of using charts and other recording methods to analyze various data in options trading. Using these visual instruments, you have the chance to determine the direction of the market because they give you a trend.

This method focuses on studying the supply and demand of a market. The price will be seen to rise when the investor realizes the market is undervalued, and this leads to buying. If they think that the market is overvalued, the prices will start falling, and this is deemed the perfect time to sell.

You need to understand the movement of the various indicators to make the perfect decision. This method works on the premise that history usually repeats itself – a huge change in the prices affects the investors in any situation.

History

Technical analysis has been used over the years in trades. The technical analysis methods have been used for over a hundred years to come up with deductions regarding the market.

In Asia, the use of technical analysis led to the development of candlestick techniques, and it forms the main charting techniques.

Over time, more tools and techniques have come up to help traders come up with predictions of the prices in various markets.

There are many indicators that you can use to determine the direction of the market, but only a few are valuable to your course. Let us look at the various indicators and how to use them.

Support and Resistance

These levels occur at points where both the buyer and the seller aren't dormant. These levels are displayed on the chart using a horizontal line extended in the past to the future.

The different prices reach at the support and resistance points in the future.

How to Apply Support and Resistance

- Using these points allows you to know when to call or put.

- Support and resistance give you a way to determine the entry point to use for a directional trade.

The Significance of Trends in Option Trading

Technical analysis works on the premise of the trend. These trends come by due to the interaction of the buyer and the seller. The aggressiveness of one of the parties in the market will determine how steep the trend becomes. To make a profit, you have to take advantage of the changes in the price movement.

To understand the direction of the trend, you ought to look at the troughs and peaks and how they relate to each other.

When looking for money in options trading, you ought to trade with a trend. The trend is what determines the decision you make when faced with a situation – whether to buy or to sell. You need to know the various signs that a prevailing trend is soon ending so that you can manage the risks and exit the trades the right way.

Characteristics of Technical Analysis

This analysis makes use of models and trading rules using different price and volume changes. These include the volume, price, and other different market info.

Technical analysis is applied among financial professionals and traders and is used by many option traders.

The Principles of Technical analysis

Many traders on the market use the price to come up with information that affects the decision you make ultimately. The analysis looks at the trading pattern and what information it offers you rather than looking at drivers such as news events, economic and fundamental events.

Price action usually tends to change every time because the investor leans towards a certain pattern, which in turn predicts trends and conditions.

Prices Determine Trends

Technical analysts know that the price in the market determines the trend of the market. The trend can be up, down, or move sideways.

History Usually Repeats Itself

Analysts believe that an investor repeats the behavior of the people that traded before them. The investor sentiment usually repeats itself. Due to the fact that the behavior repeats itself, traders know that using a price pattern can lead to predictions.

The investor uses the research to determine if the trend will continue or if the reversal will stop eventually and will anticipate a change when the charts show a lot of investor sentiment.

Combination with Other Analysis Methods

To make the most out of the technical analysis, you need to combine it with other charting methods on the market. You also need to use secondary data, such as sentiment analysis and indicators.

To achieve this, you need to go beyond pure technical analysis, and combine other market forecast methods in line with technical work. You can use technical analysis along with fundamental analysis to improve the performance of your portfolio.

You can also combine technical analysis with economics and quantitative analysis. For instance, you can use neural networks along with technical analysis to identify the relationships in the market. Other traders make use of technical analysis with astrology.

Other traders go for newspaper polls, sentiment indicators to come with deductions.

The Different Types of Charts Used in Technical Analysis

Candlestick Chart

This is a charting method that came from the Japanese. The method fills the interval between opening and closing prices to show a relationship. These candles use color coding to show the closing points. You will come across black, red, white, blue, or green candles to represent the closing point at any time.

Open-high-low-close Chart (OHLC)

These are also referred to as bar charts, and they give you a connection between the maximum and minimum prices in a trading period. They usually feature a tick on the left side to show the open price and one on the right to show the closing price.

Line Chart

This is a chart that maps the closing price values using a line segment.

Point and Figure Chart

This employs numerical filters that reference times without fully using the time to construct the chart.

Overlays

These are usually used on the main price charts and come in different ways:
- Resistance – refers to a price level that acts as the maximum level above the usual price
- Support – the opposite of resistance, and it shows as the lowest value of the price
- Trend line – this is a line that connects two troughs or peaks.
- Channel – refers to two trend lines that are parallel to each other
- Moving average – a kind of dynamic trendline that looks at the average price in the market
- Bollinger bands – these are charts that show the rate of volatility in a market.
- Pivot point – this refers to the average of the high, low, and closing price averages for a certain stock or currency.

Price-based Indicators

These analyze the price values of the market. These include:
- Advance decline line – this is an indicator of the market breadth

- Average directional index – shows the strength of a trend in the market
- Commodity channel index – helps you to identify cyclical trends in the market
- Relative strength index – this is a chart that shows you the strength of the price
- Moving average convergence (MACD) – this shows the point where two trend line converge or diverge.
- Stochastic oscillator – this shows the close position that has happened within the recent trading range
- Momentum – this is a chart that tells you how fast the price changes

The Benefits of Technical Analysis in Options Trading

There are a variety of benefits that you enjoy when you use technical analysis in trading options. The benefits arise from the fact that traders are usually asking a lot of questions touching on the price of the market and entry points. While the forecast for prices is a huge task, the use of technical analysis makes it easier to handle.

The major advantages of technical analysis include

Expert Trend Analysis

This is the biggest advantage of technical analysis in any market. With this method, you can predict the direction of the market at any time. You can determine whether the market will move up, down or sideways easily.

Entry and Exit Points

As a trader, you need to know when to place a trade and when to opt out. The entry point is all about knowing the right time to enter the trade for good returns. Exiting a trade is also vital because it allows you to reduce losses.

Leverage Early Signals

Every trader looks for ways to get early signals to assist them in making decisions. Technical analysis gives you signals to trigger a decision on your part. This is usually ideal when you suspect that a trend will reverse soon. Remember the time the trend reverses are when you need to make crucial decisions.

It Is Quick

In options trading, you need to go with techniques that give you fast results. Additionally, getting technical analysis data is cheaper than other techniques in fundamental analysis, with some companies offering free charting programs. If you are in the market to make use of short time intervals such as 1-minute, 5-minute, 30 minute or 1-hour charts, you can get this using technical analysis.

It Gives You A Lot of Information

Technical analysis gives you a lot of information that you can use to make trading decisions. You can easily build a position depending on the information you get then take or exit trades. You have access to information such as chart pattern, trends, support, resistance, market momentum, and other information. The current price of an asset usually reflects every known information of an asset. While the market might be rife with rumors that the prices might surge or plummet, the current price represents the final point for all information. As the traders and investors change their bearing from one part to another, the changes in asset reflect the current value perception.

If all this turns out to be true, then the only info you require is a price chart that gives all the price reflections and predictions. There isn't any need for you to worry yourself with the reasons why the price is rising or falling when you can use a chart to determine everything.

With the right technical analysis information, you can make trading easier and faster because you make decisions based not on hearsay but facts. You don't have to spend your time reading and trying to make headway in financial news. All you need us to check what the chart tells you.

You Understand Trends

If the prices on the market were to gyrate randomly without any direction, you would find it hard to make money. While these trends run in all directions, the prices always move in trends. Directional bias allows you to leverage the benefits of making money. Technical analysis allows you to determine when a trend occurs and when it doesn't occur, or when it is in reversal.

Many of the profitable techniques that are used by the traders to make money follow trends. This means that you find the right trend and then look for opportunities that allow you to enter the market in the same direction as the trend. This helps you to capitalize on the price movement.

Trends run in various degrees. The degree of the trend determines how much money you make, whether in the short term or long-term trading. Technical analysis gives you all the tools that make it possible for you to do this.

History Always Repeats Itself

Technical analysis uses common patterns to give you the information to trade. However, you need to understand that history will not be exact when it repeats itself, though. The current analysis will be either bigger or smaller, depending on the existing market conditions. The only thing is that it won't be a replica of the prior pattern.

This pans out easily because most human psychology doesn't change so much, and you will see that the emotions have a hand in making sure that prices rise and fall. The emotions that traders exhibit create a lot of patterns that lead to changes in prices all the time. As a trader, you need to identify these patterns and then use them for trading. Use prior history to guide you and then the current price as a trigger of the trade.

Enjoy Proper Timing

Do you know that without proper timing you will not be able to make money at all? One of the major advantages of technical analysis is that you get the chance to time the trades. Using technical analysis, you get to wait, then place your money in other opportunities until it is the right time to place a trade.

Applicable Over a Wide Time Frame

When you learn technical analysis, you get to apply it to many areas in different markets, including options. All the trading in a market is based mostly on the patters that are as a result of human behavior. These patterns can then be mapped out on a chart to be used across the markets.

While there is some difference between analyzing different securities, you will be able to use technical analysis in most of the markets.

Additionally, you can use the analysis in any timeframe, which is applicable whether you use hourly, daily, or weekly charts. These markets are usually taken to be fractal, which essentially means that patterns that appear on a small scale will also be present on a large scale as well.

Technical Analysis Secrets to Become the Best Trader

To make use of technical analysis the right way, you need to follow time-testing approaches that have made the technique a gold mine for many traders. Let us look at the various tips that will take you from novice to pro in just a few days:

Use More than One Indicator

Numbers make trading easy, but it also applies to the way you apply your techniques. For one, you need to know that just because one technical indicator is better than using one, applying a second indicator is better than using just one. The use of more than one indicator is one of the best ways to confirm a trend. It also increases the odds of being right.

As a trader, you will never be 100 percent right at all times, and you might even find that the odds are stashed against you when everything is plain to see. However, don't demand too much from your indicators such that you end up with analysis paralysis.

To achieve this, make use of indicators that complement each other rather than the ones that clash against each other.

Go For Multiple Time Frames

Using the same buy signal every day allows you to have confidence that the indicator is giving you all you need to know to trade. However, make sure you look for a way to use multiple timeframes to confirm a trend. When you have a doubt, it is wise that you increase the timeframe from an hour to a day or from a daily chart to a weekly chart.

Understand that No Indicator Measures Everything

You need to know that indicators are supposed to show how strong a trend is, they won't tell you much more. So, you need to understand and focus on what the indicator is supposed to communicate instead of working with assumptions.

Go With the Trend

If you notice that an option is trading upward, then go ahead and buy it. Conversely when the trend stops trending, then it is time to sell it. If you aren't sure of what is going on in the market at that time, then don't make a move.

However, waiting might make you lose profitable trades as opposed to trading. You also miss out on opportunities to create more capital.

Have the Right Skills

It really takes superior analytical capabilities and real skill to be successful at trading, just like any other endeavor. Many people think that it is hard to make money with options trading, but with the right approach, you can make extraordinary profits.

You need to learn and understand the various skills so that you know what the market seeks from you and how to achieve your goals.

Trade with a Purpose

Many traders go into options trading with the main aim of having a hobby. Well, this way you won't be able to make any money at all. What you need to do is to trade for the money – strive to make profits unlike those who try to make money as a hobby.

Always Opt for High value

Well, no one tells you to trade any security that comes your way – it is purely a matter of choice. Try and go for high-value options so that you can trade them the right way. Make use of fundamental analysis to choose the best options to trade in.

Be Disciplined

When using technical analysis, you might find yourself in situations that require you to make a decision fast. To achieve success, you need to have strict risk management protocols. Don't base on your track record to come up with choices; instead, make sure you follow what the analysis tells you.

Don't Overlook Your Trading Plan

The trading plan is in place to guide you when things go awry. Coming up with the plan is easy, but many people find it hard to implement the plan the right way. The trading plan has various components – the signals and the take-profit/stop-loss rules. Once you get into the market, you need to control yourself because you have already taken a leap. Remember you cannot control the indicators once they start running – all you can do is to prevent yourself from messing up everything.

Come up with the trading rules when you are unemotional to try and mitigate the effects of making bad decisions.

Accept Losses

Many people trade with one thing in mind – losses aren't part of their plan. This is a huge mistake because you need to understand that every trade has two sides to it – a loss and a profit. Remember that the biggest mistake that leads to losses isn't anything to do with bad indicators rather using them the wrong way. Always have a stop-loss order when you trade to prevent loss of money.

Have a Target When You Trade

So, what do you plan to achieve today? Remember, trading is a way to grow your capital as opposed to saving. Options trading is a business that has probable outcomes that you get to estimate. When you make a profit, make sure you take some money from the table and then put it in a safe place.

How to Apply Technical Analysis

Many traders have heard of technical analysis, but they don't know how to use it to make deductions and come up with decisions that impact their trades. Here are the different steps to make sure you have the right decision when you use technical analysis.

1.   Identify a Trend

You need to identify an option and then see whether there is a trend or not. The trend might be driving the options up or down. The market is bullish if it is moving up and bearish when it is moving down. As a trader, you need to go along with the trend instead of fighting it. When you fight against the trend, you incur unnecessary losses that will make it hard to achieve the rewards that you seek.

You also need to have good ways to identify the trend; this is because the market has the capacity to move in a certain direction. It is not all about identifying the direction of the trend but also when the trend is moving out of the trend.

So, how can you identify a trend the right way? Here are some tools to use so as to get the right trend:
- Using triangles that map major swings
- The Bill Williams Fractals indicator helps you to identify the trend
- Use the moving average
- Trend lines give you an idea of the direction of the trend

Once you identify the trend, the next step is to try and mark the support and resistance levels

2. Support and Resistance Levels

You need to understand the support and resistance levels that are within the trend. Use the Fibonacci retracement tool to identify these spots on the trend.

3. Look for Patterns

Patterns need to show you what to expect in a certain market. You can use candlesticks to determine the chart pattern.

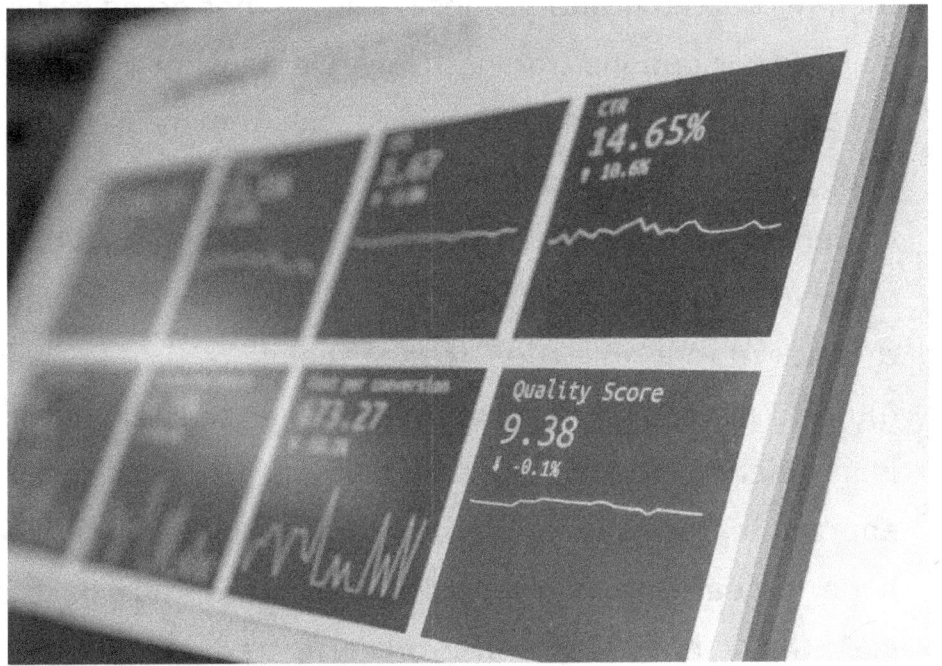

Chapter 9   Trading psychology

Options prices can move a lot over the course of short time periods. So someone who likes to see their money protected and not losing any is not going to be suitable for options trading. Now, we all want to come out ahead, so I am not saying that you have to be happy about losing money in order to be an options trader. What you have to be willing to do is calmly observe your options losing money, and then be ready to stick it out in order to see gains return in the future. This is akin to riding a real roller coaster, but it is a financial roller coaster. Options do not slowly appreciate the way a Warren Buffett investor would hope to see. Options move big on a percentage basis, and they move fast. If you are trading multiple contracts at once, you might see yourself losing $500 and then earning $500 over a matter of a few hours. In this sense, although most options traders are not "day traders" technically speaking, you will be better off if you have a little bit of a day trading mindset.

Getting it all started

You may be excited to jump into the market and start trading right away, but there are a few things that you will need to do first. You will need to start out with a good understanding of the basics that come with options and you need to know some of the option types that you can pick from. We talked about these topics a little bit before, but the more that you can learn about them before investing, the more success you will have.

After you have had some time to understand what options are all about and what you will be getting yourself into, it is time to come up with your motivation for trading. Ask yourself how much money you are looking to make from this trade and how you would like to use that money when you have earned it. This motivation is going to help you out so much when you are in the thick of the trading and you need some help staying focus.

The trading plan is going to basically list all of the things that you want to be able to accomplish while you are trading. It can include what you expect to happen, some of your goals, the strategy that you will go with, and any other guidelines that will help you be successful. Those who decide to start investing in options without having a good plan in place will be the ones who run into a lot of risks.

You don't make emotional decisions

Since options are, by their nature, volatile, and very volatile for many stocks, coming to options trading and being really emotional about it is not a good way to approach your trading. If you are emotional, you are going to exit your trades at the wrong time in 75% of cases. You don't want to make any sudden moves when it comes to trading options. As we have said, you should have a trading plan with rules on exiting your positions, stick to those rules and you should be fine.

Be a little bit math-oriented

In order to really understand options trading and be successful, you cannot be shy about numbers. Options trading is a numbers game. That doesn't mean you have to drive over to the nearest university and get a statistics degree. But if you do understand probability and statistics, you are going to be a better options trader. Frankly, it's hard to see how you can be a good options trader without having a mind for numbers. Some math is at the core of options trading and you cannot get around it.

You are market-focused

You don't have to set up a day trading office with ten computer screens so you can be tracking everything by the moment, but if you are hoping to set up a trade and lazily come back to check it three days later, that isn't going to work with options trading. You do need to be checking your trades a few times a day. You also need to be keeping up with the latest financial and economic news, and you need to keep up with any news directly related to the companies you invest in or any news that could impact those companies. If the news does come out, you are going to need to make decisions if it's news that isn't going to be favorable to your positions. Also, you need to be checking the charts periodically so you have an idea of where things are heading for now.

Keep detailed trading journals

You don't want to get in the same situation with your options trading. It can be an emotional experience because trading options is active and fast-paced. When you have a profitable trade, it will be exciting. But you need to keep a journal to record all of your trades, in order to know exactly what the real situation is. That doesn't mean you quit if you look at your journal and find out you have a losing record, what you do is figure out why your trades aren't profitable and then make adjustments.

Take a disciplined approach

Don't just buy options for a certain stock because it feels good. You need to do research on your stocks. That will include doing fundamental analysis. This is going to mean paying attention to the history of a stock, knowing what the typical ranges are for, stock in recent history is, and also reading through the company's financial statements and prospectus.

Select a Security

This can be done by researching the finance sections of major news corporations. New options traders, and particularly those who are new to trading in general, should approach options trading cautiously. Rather than diving right in, investors should get their feet wet by experimenting with a limited number of securities and options so that they can keep track of gains and losses and avoid mistakes for future investments.

Choose OTC or Regulated

Trading While this can be decided at a later stage, it is suggested here so that new investors can refer to the boards of a regulated exchange, such as the New York Stock Exchange, when choosing a put or call that is well suited to their tastes. Practiced traders can pick up an OTC option later if desired, such as a call to cover the cost of an insurance put, also known as a married put.

Select Strategies

Before beginning trading, investors will need to be sure they are familiar with a few simple strategies that can be implemented with a stock.

Examine the Market

Investors will need to study the time frame charts associated with their underlying security selection.

Purchase Options and Trade

Based upon conclusions drawn from studying time frame charts, investors will need to buy the appropriate calls or puts. At the same time, investors should choose one or two of the strategies with which they are already familiar that they believe will work well in the present market climate. If trading via a regulated exchange, options for the strategies may be selected from a list published by the exchange.

Utilizing options for trading purposes

Options can generally be utilized for trading purposes in one of two ways. First, they can be used as a type of speculation whereby those who believe they are in the know can test out their hypothesis without committing fully to their hunch.

Alternatively, those who are already flush with underlying assets can then use options trading as a type of insurance if they are unsure how some of their other investments are going to perform in either the short or the long term. Typically, options are purchased when major losses on riskier investments are expected in the near future as they allow the holder to wait and see how things proceed before getting a fair price for their investment no matter how the market falls.

Appreciate That Options Trading Is Not Simple

It is vital at this stage to recapitulate the meaning of options trading. This is a contract that grants one the right of either buying or selling a security based on the speculative value of it in a limited period of time. However, the contract is not obligatory in nature. In understanding options trading, two forms of it have to be understood; first is a call option, and the other is the put option. The two are opposites of each other. One buys the former option when one expects an asset's value to go up over time but before the deadline of expiry of the contract expires.

Read and Understand Essential Literature Available On Options Trading

Reading is part of the process of educating one's self in business. A lot of literature is currently available on various platforms for the benefit of those seeking to understand investments and avenues of investment. Success and failure stories are also hugely available, particularly on the internet where people could acquire first-hand accounts on the options trading venture.

However, reading is only helpful if the correct material is being read. Not every account of business success stories is true. Some are exaggerated while others are written to arouse interest to influence people into making certain decisions for business purposes. The internet is full of hidden business activities, some of which are even hidden behind the sensational headlines of the literature resources striking people's eyes on their phones and computers. This means that knowledge is only good when it comes from the correct source.

Acquire an Understanding of the Basics of the Kinds of Trades

The trades are basically either a call option or the put option. These have to be understood well since they are the start of knowing this trade as an investment. The types of trade are the core part of the knowledge that a person can gain on options trading. All these can be explained with a desire to gain an understanding of how each of the two types of trades works. This can be achieved the desire for understanding can involve seeking mentorship or seeking consultancy firm. It can call for some level of schooling in order to begin to attain literacy, especially for those people who did not have prior knowledge of economic investments.

An options trading mindset

When it comes to making money trading options, it is important to remember that you must control your emotions at all times, something that is easier said than done, especially if you are in the moment and have just taken an unexpected loss. Cultivating the proper mindset can be done with practice, however, and doing so will make it easier for you to face the early parts of your options trading career with the proper expectations in regards to what sort of results you can expect from options trading. Specifically, this means that you will need to understand that investing in options isn't a quick and easy path to success and, rather, is sure to take plenty of dedication and hard work if you hope to see reap the potential rewards.

The first step to finding success via options trading is to get your emotions in check. The best traders are robotic, they only rely on the facts and they follow their trading plan 100 percent of the time. If you find yourself getting extremely emotional as far as trading is concerned then it is important that you start off by keeping a log of the emotions you have while trading, and the results of those emotions on your trading outcome. While this might seem unnecessary at first, you will be surprised how helpful having a clear outline of your personal patterns is when it comes to improving your overall trade percentage in the long term.

The fact of the matter is that if you ever hope to successfully trade options then you are going to need to know you can stick with your plan no matter what the emotional part of your mind is telling you to do. A good plan is one that remains successful, not 100 percent of the time, or even 95 percent of the time and instead manages to be successful roughly 60 percent of the time. While 60 percent is certainly enough to ensure you turn a profit, it is not enough that it allows for additional wiggle room in the terms of letting your emotions talking you into going off book at every turn. Remember, trading options is a numbers game and keeping your emotions in check is key to not working with skewed data.

Setting up a reasonable expectation

A trader who is staring up should always have the patience to wait to know a market and should not expect that he or she would large and handsome profit from their trading options. A new trader should never high expectation when they are just into the market. Rather they should be mentally prepared for losing capital rather than gaining capital. A trader should always begin to expect at least at a minimum market experience of a year or half. This can be illustrated very simply in any field. A famous successful person always bears time and patience to be the greatest achiever in their field.

Proof concept

If a trader starts off with the small trade he or she will not only gain experience but will also save time. Noises of the stock market do not affect the small traders but if a trader starts with big trading options he or she will react to these noises in the stock market. A new trader will be in a bad situation with such reactions and at the early time period. Starting with a small trade will teach a trader to manage capital which is very much necessary. A trader remembers all trades are not same in nature. A good trader will generate great ideas after the proper experience. A trader must always have records and check on them to see what idea works for them and what does not.

Proper sorting and record keeping

A good successful trader should always keep a record of few important things of the market like:
- The trader should keep a record of orders placed and quantity involved in it and money making out of it.

- The trader should keep in mind implied volatility and its reference to current condition.

- The trader should keep in mind about his competitors in the market in that particular trade.

- When the traders begin to keep a record and maintain records they begin to move towards success and chances of being in odd position is also reduced.

Good position of the trader

Once a trader has achieved his or her position in a trade or stock market, there are frequent ups and downs. A good position trader must know how to react to these situations. By small trade, he or she won't be much affected by the noise of the stock market.
The trader should keep in mind about buying stock exchange at the perfect time. When a trader does so he or she can perfectly be in the market and understand well.

Proper evaluation of the position

A trader must decide very well that that few decisions like backing out on losses must be decided well according to perfect time.

There are few other decisions like a plan suddenly executed and whether he or she should move on with the profit or go for more?

Even if the sudden plan does not work out then he or she must have a backup and move on forward ahead and not repent on his or her loss and look for a new fresh start.

Hard work is the only way to success

It's easy to advise and listen to it. But when it comes up to the execution of the advice it's not that easy as things do not turn up the way its told.

The simple way is to start with small trade and have a lot of patience. A trader should make proper planning for execution. The trader should learn about the market and get into a good position and stick well to it and work very hard to achieve success and be a good disciplined successful trader.

At this point, it is time to move on to the next step. You already know some of the basics that come with working on options as well as some of their benefits.

Chapter 10

The Best Strategies to Make Money

Good strategies of any kind of options trading are the major key to any kind of success that is about to be unfolded in any activity. Strategies are normally laid in the trading plan and should be strictly implemented in every options trading move that is likely to be involved. Let us wholly venture into the best strategies so far in options trading.

1. Collars. The collar strategy is established by holding a number of shares of the underlying stock available in the market where protective puts are bought and the call options sold. In this kind of strategy, the options trader is likely to really protect his or her capital used in the trading activities rather than the idea of acquiring more money during trading. This kind is considered conservative and rather much more important in options trading.

2. Credit spreads. It is presumed that the biggest fear of most traders is a financial breakdown. In this side of strategy, the trader gets to sell one put and then buy another one.
3. Covered calls. Covered calls are a good kind of strategy where a particular trader sells the right for another trader to purchase his or her stock at some strike price and get to gain a good amount of cash. However, there is a specific time that this strategy should be utilized and in a case where the buyer fails to purchase some of the stock and the expiration date dawns, the contract becomes invalid right away.
4. Cash naked put. Cash naked put is a kind of strategy where the options trader gets to write at the money or out of the money during a particular trading activity and aligning some particular amount of money aside for the purpose of purchasing stock.
5. Long call strategy. This is the most basic strategy in options trading and the one that is quite easy to comprehend. In the long call strategy for options trading, aggressive

option traders who happen to be bullish are pretty much involved. This implies that bullish options traders end up buying stock during the trading activities with the hope of it rising in the near future. The reward is unlimited in the long call strategy.

6. Short call option strategy. The short call strategy is the reverse of the long call one. Bearish kind of traders is so aggressive in the falling out of stock prices during trading in this kind of strategy. They decide to sell the call options available. This move is considered to be so risky by the experienced options traders believing that prices may drastically decide to rise once again. This significantly implies that large chunks of losses are likely to be incurred, leading to a real downfall of your trading structure and everything involved in it.

7. Long put option strategy. First things first, you should be contented that buying a put is the opposite of buying a call. So in this kind of strategy, when you become bearish, that is the moment you may purchase a put option. Put option puts the trader in a

situation where he can sell his stock at a particular period of time before the expiration date is reached. This strategy exposes the trader to a mere kind of risk in the options trading market.

8. Trading time. It is depicted that options trading for a longer period is much value as compared to a short period dating. The longer the trading day, the more skills and knowledge the trader is likely to be engaged into as he or she is likely to get the adequate experience that is needed for good trading. Mastering good trading moves for a while gives the trader the experience and adequate skills.

9. Bull call spread strategy. In this kind of strategy, the investor gets to purchase several calls at a particular strike price and then purchases the price at a much higher price. The calls always bear a similar expiration date and come from the same underlying stock. This type of strategy is mostly implemented by the bullish options traders.

10. Bear put strategy. This strategy involves a trader purchasing put options at a particular price amount and later selling off at a lower price amount. These options bear a similar expiration date and from the same underlying stock. This strategy is mostly utilized by traders who are said to be bearish. The consequences are limited losses and limited gains.

11. Iron condor. The iron condor involves the bull call spread strategy and the bear put strategy all at the same time during a particular trading period. The expiration dates of the stock are still similar and are of the same underlying stock. Most traders get to use this strategy when the market is expected to experience low volatility rates and with the expectation of gaining a little amount of premium. Iron condor works in both up and down markets are is really believed to be economical during the up and down markets.

12. Married put strategy. On this end, the options trader purchase options at a particular amount of money and at the same time, get to buy the same number of shares of the underlying stock. This kind of strategy is also known as the

protective put. This is also a bearish kind of options trading strategy.

13. Cash covered put strategy. Here, one or more contracts are sold with a 100 shares multiplied with the strike price amount for every particular contract involved in the options trading. Most traders use this strategy to acquire an extra amount of premium on a specific stock they would wish to purchase.

14. Long or short calendar spread strategy. This is a tricky type of strategy. The market stock is said to be stagnant, not moving and waiting for the right timing until the expiration of the front-month is reached.

15. Synthetic long arbitrage strategy. Most traders take advantage of this strategy when they are trying to take advantage of the different market prices in different kinds of markets with just the same property.

16. Put ratio back spread strategy. This is a bearish type of options strategy where the trader gets to sell some put options and gets to purchase more options of just the same underlying stock with a similar expiration date and a lower price.

17. Call ratio back spread. In this strategy, the trader uses both the long and short options positions so as to eradicate consistent losses and target achieving large loads of benefits over a particular trading period. The essence of this strategy is to generate profits in case the stock prices tend to elevate and reduce the number of risks likely to be involved. This strategy is mostly implemented by bullish kind of options traders.

18. Long butterfly strategy. This strategy involves three parts where one put option is purchased at particular and then selling the other two options at a price lower than the buying price and purchasing one put at even lower price during a particular trading period.

19. Short butterfly strategy. In this strategy, three parts are still involved where a put option is sold at a much higher price and two puts are then purchased at a lower price than the purchase price and a put option is later on sold at a much lower strike price. In both cases, all put bear the same expiration date and the strike prices are normally equidistant as revealed in various options

trading charts. A short butterfly strategy is the reverse way of the long butterfly strategy.

20. Long straddle. The long straddle is also known as the buy strangle where a slight pull and a slight call are purchased during a particular period before the expiration date reaches. The importance of this strategy is that the trader bears a large chance of acquiring good amounts of profits during his or her trading time before the expiration date is achieved.

21. Short straddle. In this kind of strategy, the trader sells both the call and put options at a similar price and bearing the same expiration date. Traders practice this strategy with the hope of acquiring good amounts of profits and experience limited various kinds of risks.

22. Owning positions that are already in a portfolio. Most traders prefer purchasing and selling various options that already hedge existing positions. This kind of strategy method is believed to incur good profits and incur losses too in other occurrences.

23. Albatross trade strategy. This kind of strategy aims at gaining some amounts of profits when the market is stagnant during a specific

options trading period or a pre-determined period of time. This kind of strategy is similar to the short gut strategy.

24. Reverse iron condor strategy. This kind of strategy focuses on benefiting some profits when the underlying stock in the current market dares to make some sharp market trade moves in either direction. Eventually, a limited amount of risks are experienced and a limited amount of profits during trading.

25. Iron butterfly spread. Buying and holding four different options in the market at three different market prices is involved in the trading market for a particular trading period.

26. Short bull ratio strategy. Short bull ratio strategy is used to benefit from the amounts of profits gained from increasing security involved in the trading market in a similar way in which we normally get to buy calls during a particular period.

27. Bull condor spread. This is a type of strategy that is designed to return a profit if the actual price of security decides to rise to a predicted price range during a specific trading period impacting good chunks of profits made to

the options trader and a limited number of risks involved.

28. Put ratio spread strategy. This strategy entails purchasing a number of put options and adding more options with various strike prices and equal kind of underlying stock during a particular options trading period.

29. Strap straddle strategy. Strap straddle strategy uses one put and two calls bearing a similar strike price and with an equal date of expiration and also containing the same underlying stock that is normally stagnant during a particular trading period. The trader utilizes this type of strategy for the hope of getting higher amounts of profits as compared to the regular straddle strategy over a particular period of the trading period.

30. Strap strangle strategy. This strategy is bullish, where more call options are purchased as compared to the put options and a bullish inclination is then depicted in various trading charts information.

31. Put back spread strategy. This back spread strategy combines both the short puts

and long puts so as to establish a position where the ratio of losses and profits entirely depends on the ratio of their two puts that are likely to be experienced in the market.

32. Short call ratio. This strategy involves purchasing a single call and later on selling two other calls at a higher price amount during a specific period of time before its expiration. This concept combines the protocols of the bull call spread strategy and the naked call strategy. The essence of this strategy is to acquire limited loss potential and mixed profits potential to the options trader involved during a particular period of time.

33. Iron albatross strategy. The particular trader gets to use this type of strategy when expecting a particular underlying stock to trade during a particular period of time before expiration. Four transactions are usually involved in this strategy and a high level of trading is called for. This implies that this measure kind is so suitable for the experienced traders, ones who have mastered almost every market move.

34. Bull call ladder spread strategy. This one is almost similar to the bull call strategy where security increasing in price is

expected to source out some profits to the trader during options trading.

Chapter 11 Tips for Success

As already noted, options simply involve putting a price on the possibility or probability that a future event will take place. If an event is likely to actually happen, then that particular option related to that event becomes very expensive. Therefore, the more likely an event is, the better the profits from the option.

It is important to learn how to trade in options because it offers a reliable and long-term source of income. Many investors have generated wealth and become prosperous by simply trading in stock options. Options are a preferred means of investment because of various reasons. One of these is the relatively low cost of investment required. As an investor, you do not need large sums of money to buy options. They are very cheaply priced yet they offer rewards that are just as good as those enjoyed by investors in the stocks markets.

There have been plenty of advances made, over the last couple of decades, on how commodity markets function. One of the most notable of these advances is the development of online trading platforms and the speed at which deals are concluded. Trading online is fast, easy and convenient. It enables any interested investor to open an account through a broker and then start trading options and earn good returns as soon as is practically possible.

Options trading present a new, more advanced method of investing. To be successful in options trading, it is very important that you understand exactly what you are doing. This will ensure that you are not just an amateur groping in the dark but a true investor.

One of the most important reasons why trade in options is gaining popularity is that investors do not need to invest large sums of money as compared to those investing directly in stocks and shares. This is because traders do not need to actually buy the underlying stocks or shares but simply the rights affiliated with the options. However, the returns are just as great, if not greater, as those gotten from trade in securities.

Options require an arsenal of successful methods and tactics to be profitable. For a beginner or the average investor, a powerful and successful strategy is definitely essential. Whenever you invest money in the stock market, always diversify your portfolio and if possible, include options. This way, you will greatly increase the income that you derive from your investments.

Succeeding on Calls

Know when to go off book: While sticking to your plan, even when your emotions are telling you to ignore it, is the mark of a successful trader, this in no way means that you must blindly follow your plan 100 percent of the time. You will, without a doubt, find yourself in a situation from time to time where your plan is going to be rendered completely useless by something outside of your control. You need to be aware enough of your plan's weaknesses, as well as changing market conditions, to know when following your predetermined course of action is going to lead to failure instead of success. Knowing when the situation really is changing, versus when your emotions are trying to hold sway is something that will come with practice, but even being aware of the disparity is a huge step in the right direction.

Avoid trades that are out of the money: While there are a few strategies out there that make it a point of picking up options that are currently out of the money, you can rest assured that they are most certainly the exception, not the rule. Remember, the options market is not like the traditional stock market which means that even if you are trading options based on underlying stocks buying low and selling high is just not a viable strategy.

If a call has dropped out of the money, there is generally less than a 10 percent chance that it will return to acceptable levels before it expires which means that if you purchase these types of options what you are doing is little better than gambling, and you can find ways to gamble with odds in your favor of much higher than 10 percent.

Avoid hanging on too tightly to your starter strategy: That doesn't mean that it is the last strategy that you are ever going to need, however, far from it. Your core trading strategy is one that should always be constantly evolving as the circumstances surrounding your trading habits change and evolve as well. What's more, outside of your primary strategy you are going to want to eventually create additional plans that are more specifically tailored to various market states or specific strategies that are only useful in a narrow band of situations. Remember, the more prepared you are prior to starting a day's worth of trading, the greater your overall profit level is likely to be, it is as simple as that.

Utilize the spread: If you are not entirely risk averse, then when it comes to taking advantage of volatile trades the best thing to do is utilize a spread as a way of both safeguarding your existing investments and, at the same time, making a profit. To utilize a long spread you are going to want to generate a call and a put, both with the same underlying asset, expiration details, and share amounts but with two very different strike prices. The call will need to have a higher strike price and will mark the upper limit of your profits and the put will have a lower strike price that will mark the lower limit of your losses. When creating a spread it is important that you purchase both halves at the same time as doing it in fits and spurts can add extraneous variables to the formula that are difficult to adjust for properly.

Never proceed without knowing the mood of the market: While using a personalized trading plan is always the right choice, having one doesn't change the fact that it is extremely important to consider the mood of the market before moving forward with the day's trades. First and foremost, it is important to keep in mind that the collective will of all of the traders who are currently participating in the market is just as much as a force as anything that is more concrete, including market news. In fact, even if companies release good news to various outlets and the news is not quite as good as everyone was anticipating it to be then related prices can still decrease.

To get a good idea of what the current mood of the market is like, you are going to want to know the average daily numbers that are common for your market and be on the lookout for them to start dropping sharply. While a day or two of major fluctuation can be completely normal, anything longer than that is a sure sign that something is up. Additionally, you will always want to be aware of what the major players in your market are up to.

Never get started without a clear plan for entry and exit: While finding your first set of entry/exit points can be difficult without experience to guide you, it is extremely important that you have them locked down prior to starting trading, even if the stakes are relatively low. Unless you are extremely lucky, starting without a clear idea of the playing field is going to do little but lose your money. If you aren't sure about what limits you should set, start with a generalized pair of points and work to fine tune it from there.

More important than setting entry and exit points, however, is using them, even when there is still the appearance of money on the table. One of the biggest hurdles that new options traders need to get over is the idea that you need to wring every last cent out of each and every successful trade. The fact of the matter is that, as long as you have a profitable trading plan, then there will always be more profitable trades in the future which means that instead of worrying about a small extra profit you should be more concerned with protecting the profit that the trade has already netted you. While you may occasionally make some extra profit ignoring this advice, odds are you will lose far more than you gain as profits peak unexpectedly and begin dropping again before you can effectively pull the trigger. If you are still having a hard time with this concept, consider this: options trading is a marathon, not a sprint, slow and steady will always win the race.

Never double down: When they are caught up in the heat of the moment, many new options traders will find themselves in a scenario where the best way to recoup a serious loss is to double down on the underlying stock in question at its newest, significantly lowered, price in an effort to make a profit under the assumption that things are going to turn around and then continue to do so to the point that everything is completely profitable once again. While it can be difficult to let an underlying stock that was once extremely profitable go, doubling down is rarely if ever going to be the correct decision. If you find yourself in a spot where you don't know if the trade you are about to make is actually going to be a good choice, all you need to do is ask yourself if you would make the same one if you were going into the situation blind, the answer should tell you all you need to know.

If you find yourself in a moment where doubling down seems like the right choice, you are going to need to have the strength to talk yourself back down off of that investing ledge and to cut your losses as thoroughly as possible given the current situation. The sooner you cut your losses and move on from the trade that ended poorly, the sooner you can start putting energy and investments into a trade that still has the potential to make you a profit.

Never take anything personally: It is human nature to build stories around, and therefore form relationships with, all manner of inanimate objects including individual stocks or currency pairs. This is why it is perfectly natural to feel a closer connection to particular trades, and possibly even consider throwing out your plan when one of them takes an unexpected dive. Thinking about and acting on are two very different things, however, which is why being aware of these tendencies are so important to avoid them at all costs.

This scenario happens just as frequently with trades moving in positive directions as it does negative, but the results are always going to be the same. Specifically, it can be extremely tempting to hang on to a given trade much longer than you might otherwise decide to simply because it is on a hot streak that shows no sign of stopping. In these instances, the better choice of action is to instead sell off half of your shares and then set a new target based on the updated information to ensure you are in a position to have your cake and eat it too.

Not taking your choice of broker seriously: With so many things to consider, it is easy to understand why many new option traders simply settle on the first broker that they find and go about their business from there. The fact of the matter is, however, that the broker you choose is going to be a huge part of your overall trading experience which means that the importance of choosing the right one should not be discounted if you are hoping for the best experience possible. This means that the first thing that you are going to want to do is to dig past the friendly exterior of their website and get to the meat and potatoes of what it is they truly offer. Remember, creating an eye-catching website is easy, filling it will legitimate information when you have ill intent is much more difficult.

First things first, this means looking into their history of customer service as a way of not only ensuring that they treat their customers in the right way, but also of checking to see that quality of service is where it needs to be as well. Remember, when you make a trade every second count which mean that if you need to contact your broker for help with a trade you need to know that you are going to be speaking with a person who can solve your problem as quickly as possible. The best way to ensure the customer service is up to snuff is to give them a call and see how long it takes for them to get back to you. If you wait more than a single business day, take your business elsewhere as if they are this disinterested in a new client, consider what the service is going to be like when they already have you right where they want you.

With that out the way, the next thing you will need to consider is the fees that the broker is going to charge in exchange for their services. There is very little regulation when it comes to these fees which means it is definitely going to pay to shop around. In addition to fees, it is important to consider any account minimums that are required as well as any fees having to do with withdrawing funds from the account.

Find a Mentor: When you are looking to go from causal trader to someone who trades successfully on the regular, there is only so much you can learn by yourself before you need a truly objective eye to ensure you are proceeding appropriately. This person can either be someone you know in real life, or it can take the form of one or more people online. The point is you need to find another person or two who you can bounce ideas off of and whose experience you can benefit from. Options trading doesn't need to be a solitary activity; take advantage of any community you can find.

Knowledge is the key: Without some type of information which you can use to assess your trades, you are basically playing at the roulette table. Even poker players show up to the table with a game plan. They can adapt to the circumstances and learn to read other players. That way, they can tell the contenders from the pretenders. Options trading is no different. If you are unable to use the information that is out there to your advantage, then what you will end up with is a series of guesses which may or may not play out. Based purely on the law of averages you have a 50/50 chance of making money. That may not seem like bad odds, but a string of poor decisions will leave you in the poor house in no time.

So, it is crucial that you become familiar with the various analytics and tools out there which you can use to your advantage. Bear in mind that everyone is going to be looking at the same information. However, it is up to you to figure out what can, or might, happen before everyone else does. This implies really learning and studying the numbers so that you can detect patterns and see where trends are headed, or where trends may reverse. The perfect antidote to that is vision and foresight. Practice building scenarios. Try to imagine what could happen is trends continue. Or, what would happen if trends reversed? What needs to happen in order for those trends to continue or reverse?

When you ask yourself such tough questions, your knowledge and understanding begin to expand. Your mind will suddenly be able to process greater amounts of information while you generate your own contingency plans based on the multiple what ifs. That may seem like a great deal of information to handle, but at the end of the day, any time spent in improving your trading acumen is certainly worth the effort.

Mistakes to Avoid When Trading Options

Inexperienced traders are often warned away from purchasing options that are out of the money as being a greater risk than the ultimate reward is likely to be. While it is true that a short expiration time coupled with an out of the money option will frequently look appealing, especially to those with a smaller amount of trading capital to work with, the issue is that all of these types of options are likely to look equally appealing which leaves them with no way to tell the good from the bad. As a more experienced trader, however, you have many more tools at your disposal than the average novice which means that, while risky, cheap options have the potential to generate substantial returns, as long as you keep the following in mind while trading them.

Mishandling early assignment: Early assignment occurs when a holder exercises an option that you are the writer upon much early that you had anticipated, and at terms that are much less favorable than you had initially hoped. If this happens, it can be easy to become flustered and simply sell as requested, taking a loss in the process. Instead, it is important to consider all the possible options, including purchasing another option for the express purpose of selling it, to ensure that you mitigate the extra costs as completely as possible.

Ignoring the statistics behind options trading: One of the biggest mistakes that most newbie options traders make is that they forget the probability is a real thing. When you check a potential stock before purchasing an option, it's important to understand that the history of an option is important when deciding whether or not you should be investing in it, but so are the odds and probability surrounding whether or not a particular event is going to occur.

For example, a common strategy that investors use is to leverage their money by investing in cheap options so that this will help to prevent big losses on a stock that they actually own shares of. Of course, this is a good strategy, but nothing works one-hundred percent of the time. Make sure that if the rules of probability and simple ratios are telling you to stay away from a deal, you listen to the facts that are staring you in the face. Wishful thinking will come to bite you later on.

Being overzealous: Oftentimes when new options traders finally get their initial plan just right, they become overzealous and start committing to larger trades than they can realistically afford to recover from if things go poorly. It is important to take it slow when it comes to building your rate of return and never bet more than you can afford to lose. Regardless of how promising a specific trade might seem, there is not risk/reward level at which it is worth considering a loss that will take you out of the game completely for an extended period of time. Trade reasonably and trade regularly and you will see greater results in the long term guaranteed.

Not being adaptable: The successful options trades know when to follow their plans but they also know that no plan will be the right choice, even if early indicators say otherwise. There is a difference between making a point of sticking to a plan and following it blindly and knowing which is which is one of the more important indicators of the separation between options trading success and abject failure. This means it is important to be aware of when and where experimentation and new ideas are appropriate and when it is best to toe the line and gather more data in order to make a well-reasoned decision.

This also means having several different plans in your options trading tool box and not just resolutely sticking to the first one that brings you a modicum of success. This is crucial as there are certain plans that will only work in specific situations and knowing which to use when, in real time, will lead to significantly greater returns on a more reliable basis every single time.

Likewise, an adaptive options trader knows that market conditions can change unexpectedly and is prepared to respond accordingly. This means understanding when the time is right to go in a new direction, regardless of the potential risks that doing so might entail. Sometimes a good trader has to make a leap of faith, and a trader who is successful in the long term knows what signs to look for that indicate this type of scenario is occurring in real time. Unfortunately, this type of foresight cannot be taught, and instead must be found with experience.

As long as you keep the appropriate mindset regarding individual trades, any new strategy that is attempted will result in valuable data, if nothing else. It is important to understand that learning not to use a specific course of action a second time is always valuable, no matter the costs. Working to build this into your core trading mindset will lead you to greater success in a wider variety of situations in the long term.

Ignoring the probability: Always remember that the historical data will not apply to the current trends in the market at all times which means you will always want to consider the probability as well as the odds that the market is going to behave the way it typically does. The odds are how likely the market is to behave as expected and the probability is the ratio of the likelihood of a given outcome. Understanding the probability of certain outcomes can make it easy to purchase the proper options to minimize losses related to holdings of specific underlying stocks. When purchasing cheap options, it is important to remember that they are always going to be cheap for a reason as price is determined by strike price of the underlying stock as well as the amount of time remaining for the option to regain its value, choose wisely otherwise you are doing little more than gambling and there are certainly better ways to gamble than via options trading.

Letting the opinions of other influence your trading: While every day trader is going to have opinions regarding the best way to trade this type of stock or when to use that indicator, the best day traders tend to avoid this advice like the plague and instead work out their own. The only thing you really need to focus on in order to make the right types of trades in the right timeframes is math and anything else is only going to get in the way.

Keep in mind that you want to analyze and observe economic and political events, not get caught up in them.

Not dealing with short options properly: While, in theory, it might seem like buying back short options at the last moment is the best choice, this practice is sure to hurt your more than help you in the long run. It may be tempting to hold onto profitable options in order to squeeze the maximum return out of each investment but you need to be aware that the potential for a reversal is always lurking in the shadows. Instead, a good rule of thumb is to buy back options that are currently at 80 percent of your ideal return or higher and let the extra take care of itself. While it may hurt to leave some potential profit on the table, it will improve your overall reliability, netting you a profit in the long run.

Not considering exotic options: An exotic option is one that has a basic structure that differs from either European or American options when it comes to the how and when of how the payout will be provided or how the option relates to the underlying asset in question. Additionally, the number of potential underlying assets is going to be much more varied and can include things like what the weather is like or how much rainfall a given area has experienced. Due to the customization options and the complexity of exotic options, they are only traded over-the-counter.

While they are undoubtedly more complex to get involved with, exotic options also offer up several additional advantages when compared to common options including:

• They are a better choice for those with very specific needs when it comes to risk management.

• They offer up a variety of unique risk dimensions when it comes to both management and trading.

• They offer a far larger range of potential investments that can more easily meet a diverse number of portfolio needs.

• They are often cheaper than traditional options.

They also have additional drawbacks, the biggest of which is that they cannot often be priced correctly using standard pricing formulas. This may work as a benefit instead of a drawback, however, depending on if the mispricing falls in the favor of the trader or the writer. It is also important to keep in mind that the amount of risk that is taken on with exotic options is always going to be greater than with other options due to the limited liquidity each type of exotic option is going to have available. While some types are going to have markets that are fairly active, others are only going to have limited interest. Some are even what are known as dual-party transactions which means they have no underlying liquidity and are only traded when two amiable traders can be found.

Not keeping earnings and dividend dates in mind: It is important to keep an eye on any underlying assets that you are currently working with as those who are currently holding calls have the potential to be assigned early dividends, with greater dividends having an increased chance of this occurrence. As owning an option doesn't mean owning the underlying asset, if this happens to you then you won't be able to collect on your hard-earned money. Early assignment is largely a random occurrence which means that if you don't keep your ear to the ground it can be easy to get caught unaware and be unable to exercise the option before you miss the boat.

Along similar lines, you are going to also always want to be aware of when the earning season is going to take place for any of your underlying assets as it is likely going to increase the price of all of the contracts related to the underlying asset in question. Additionally, you will need to be caught up on current events as even the threat of influential news can be enough to cause a significant spike in volatility and premiums as well. In order to minimize the additional costs associated with trading during these periods, you are going to want to utilize a spread. Doing so will minimize the effect that inflation has on your bottom line.

Chasing bottoms and tops: There are certainly some strategies out there that are effective when used near the turning points of existing trends. These are in the minority, however, which means that picking bottoms and tops is, more often than not, a risky proposition. Unfortunately, it is an all too common mistake for traders to invest money into securities that are either too low or too high, gleefully ignoring the 2 percent rule as they do so. This impulse should be avoided like the plague and replaced with a focus on major inbound price moves instead. Sticking to one side of markets that are range-bound will lead to better long-term results at least 90 percent of the time.

Sticking with relative trends: If a trend is already well-defined in the market then it is entirely possible that it is going to continue long enough for you to make some money off of it but it is far from a guarantee. The market will naturally fluctuate up to 20 percent of its current average with very little warning, before settling back to the current standard. This means that if you recklessly jump onto a specific trend without doing the required homework you will frequently find yourself making a momentum play that is never going to go anywhere.

Before you make a move regarding a specific trend, there are three distinct timeframes you are going to want to consider first. If you are prone to trading in the short-term then you are going to want to keep an eye on the weekly hourly and daily charts. If you prefer holding onto trades for a longer period of time then daily, weekly and monthly charts are typically going to be more useful.

Conclusion

As a beginner, do not shy away from this investment. The same way you would decide to invest in a business should be the same way you should choose to engage in options trading. We can compare it to playing a chess game. Your ability to be tactical and skillful while playing is what determines the winner at the end of the game. The same applies to option trading. Your ability to reason and acquire skills will give you an added advantage over the others. How strategic can you conduct an options trading? How are you able to manage the risks involved? How do you determine the best time to carry out a trade? How do you decide on the best options to invest? How can you handle an unsuccessful business? Your answer to these questions will tell you what kind of a trader you will become. I'm making that conclusion since the concerns raised in the questions are what will determine the type of a trader you become.

We have had some people disqualifying option trading as a worthy investment. You may find that they have never engaged in any form of options trading yet they conclude it's a scam. Some may say so since they have heard from a third party, that it is not a good investment. There is a high possibility that the person invested in stocks without adequate knowledge of what it entails. As a result, they end up losing money and conclude that it was a waste of their finances. Well, I will not blame them for making such conclusions. However, their problem was based on the lack of necessary knowledge. I always say that never conclude something that you have not tried. Then again, the outcome varies among different people. You may find that a person benefits while another person does not. You never know what tomorrow hold; you could profit from an investment that another person failed in. I always encourage people to try out things by themselves and never rely on other people. If you have intended to invest in options trading, now is the time to push that desire and start trading. You might benefit significantly from it.

When you decide to engage in options trading, it is essential to note that learning never stops. There is always something new to be learned every day. There is never a time when someone can attest that there have acquired all the knowledge required. Information is diverse, and you may never manage to exhaust it fully. Take it upon yourself that you will keep learning and never get tired of doing so. As the options trading sector grows, more and more new things emerge. It will be useful if you can keep up with emerging trends. This will also influence the outcome of your earnings in options trading. You will find that the strategy that worked yesterday leads to a total loss today. If you can keep up with the emerging trends, this can be avoided. You get to adapt to the strategy that can work at that time. The constant changes will need a person who is open to change. Be willing to adapt to the changes that occur. Adopting this will enable you to maintain huge profits, minimize risks, and reduce losses.

www.ingramcontent.com/pod-product-compliance
Lightning Source LLC
Chambersburg PA
CBHW070627220526
45466CB00001B/115